All-C

Aquarium
Fishes

of the World   **John H. Prescott**

A Ridge Press Book

Bantam Books

Toronto・New York・London

Photo Credits

Alfred Castro: 65, 66, 84, 85 (top), 86, 90, 102, 103 (rt), 128, 131 (rt), 149; Sylvan Cohen: 16, 78; Ken Lucas: 33, 37, 60, 67, 68, 69 (top), 85 (btm), 105 (btm), 106 (btm), 110 (btm), 111, 114, 118, 121, 122, 131 (left), 138 (btm), 144, 145, 153; Tom McHugh: 34 (top), 61; Marineland of Florida: 31, 32, 69 (btm), 91, 101 (top), 108, 136, 141, 143; Marineland of the Pacific: 101 (btm), 103 (left); New England Aquarium: 38-39, 46-47, 106 (top), 109, 112; Aaron Norman: 41, 43, 44, 48, 50, 51, 54, 55, 56, 58, 62, 63, 64, 71, 72, 74, 77, 80, 83, 87, 88, 89, 94 (top), 96, 97, 98, 99, 115, 116, 129, 147, 150; Ontario Veterinary College: 28, 29; David C. Powell: 42, 110 (top), 154; Allan Power (Bruce Coleman): 34 (btm); John H. Prescott: 20, 105 (top left & rt), 113, 120, 123, 124, 134, 135, 138 (top & mid), 140, 146, 155; Gene Wolfsheimer: 53, 57, 59, 76, 79, 81, 94 (btm), 100, 126, 151.

Front Cover: George Sheng
Back Cover: New England Aquarium
Title Page: Royal gramma, Ken Lucas
Facing Page: New England Aquarium

Illustrations pp. 10, 11, 15, 19 by R. Lyons.

Contents

Introduction

Fishes have stimulated man's imagination for thousands of years. Although for most humans fish is primarily a food source, the Japanese and Chinese have cultured carp simply to be looked at. One variety, koi, was selectively bred to be viewed from the surface, a fact that indicates man's interest in fish-watching even before aquariums existed.

Though it is not known when the first aquarium was constructed, we do know that by 1850 the first public aquarium in the United States, the Aquarial Gardens in Boston, had been built. Several million visitors now attend public aquariums in the United States each year.

Jet aircraft have made possible the recent growth in the aquarium hobby. Millions of fishes from all over the world are now shipped to the United States. Technical improvements in equipment, tanks, and diets have also made it easier to maintain these exotic pets.

What Is a Fish ?
To maintain fishes in the home or public aquarium, it is important to recognize some basic biological characteristics. A good base of knowledge helps ensure the fishes' survival, and an understanding of their life history makes the hobby more enjoyable. A home aquarium can and should be more than a fish in a glass box.

Fishes* are a class of the subphylum of animals known as vertebrates—animals with internal skeletons and jointed backbones. The vertebrates also include the mammals, birds, reptiles, and amphibians. The most common answer to the

---

*The word "fish" can be singular or plural, but "fishes" is the correct plural when two or more species are referred to. Thus, ten guppies are ten fish because they are all of the same species, but an aquarium with ten guppies, ten tetras, and ten angel fish contains thirty fishes.

question "What is a fish?" is that it's an animal that lives in water. However, every class of vertebrates includes animals that live in or around water for all or part of their lives. Among the mammals there are the dolphins and whales, which are totally aquatic. The penguin, one of man's favorite birds, is flightless in the air but "flies" underwater. Among the reptiles, crocodiles and turtles are more at home in water than on land, and amphibians are aquatic.

Fishes are distinguished from the other vertebrates in that they possess scales, gills to extract dissolved oxygen from the water for respiration, and fins that provide propulsion and stability.

The skin of a fish, like that of all vertebrates, is composed of two layers: a thin outer epidermis and a thicker inner dermis. The scales lie between these two layers. The epidermis is so thin that it is not readily detected and is easily injured. Since the skin is an outer line of defense, a barrier between the internal and external environments, injury to this protective layer can result in infection and disease.

The gills, vital to respiration, are relatively simple structures. Like the lungs of terrestrial vertebrates, their function is to facilitate the passage of oxygen from the environment into the bloodstream, which then transports it to the body. Water is a less suitable medium for respiration than air. It is a thousand times more dense, and a given volume contains less oxygen than an equal volume of air. Fishes must expend more energy than land animals to obtain oxygen, even though gills are more efficient than lungs. Man removes only 25 percent of the available oxygen from the air he breathes, while some fishes utilize 80 percent of the available dissolved oxygen. Two **7**

Classification of Fishes*

Kingdom .... **Animalia**
Phylum .... **Chordata**
Subphylum .... **Vertebrata**
Superclass .... **Gnathostomata**
Class .... **Teleostomi**
Subclass .... **Actinopterygii**
Infraclass .... **Neopterygii**
Cohort .... **Euteleostei**
Superorder .... **Acanthopterygii**
Order .... **Perciformes**
Suborder .... **Percoidei**
Family .... **Cichlidae**
Genus .... **Pterophyllum**
Species .... **scalare**
Common Name .... **Angel Fish**

factors contribute to this efficiency. One is the structure of the gills; the other is the continuous flow of water across the gill membranes. Close examination reveals a series of double filaments attached to each curved gill arch. Each filament is folded and creased, providing greater surface area and permitting a higher rate of oxygen exchange. As water passes over the gills it is separated from the blood by a membrane through which oxygen enters the body and carbon dioxide wastes escape.

Fishes' fins are of two kinds, paired and unpaired. The

 *After Greenwood and Norman, *A History of Fishes,* 3rd ed. (N.Y.: Halsted Press, 1975).

pectoral and pelvic fins are paired; the median fins—the dorsal, anal, and caudal (or tail) fins—are unpaired. Fins are used for locomotion and stability. The median fins control movement in the longitudinal vertical axes, and the paired fins stabilize the transverse axis and control pitching and horizontal movements.

Scientists categorize and name each species of fish according to the binomial system of nomenclature. This system assigns a two-part scientific name to every living thing. The first part is the genus name, which the fish shares with its nearest relatives. The second part, the species name, is specific to the particular fish. This system helps eliminate the confusion often caused by common names. An aquarist looking for an angel fish, for example, would be confronted with both *Pterophyllum scalare,* a freshwater species, and *Holocanthus ciliaris,* a marine species. Unless he knew the correct binomial, he could not be certain of which fish he was getting.

The binomial system is based on a cascade of interrelationships. Each species belongs to a genus, each genus to a family, each family to an order, each order to a class, each class to a subphylum, and each subphylum to a phylum. An illustration of this system as applied to the freshwater angel fish, *Pterophyllum scalare,* is shown here.

The fossil record indicates that 320 to 350 million years ago fishes were the most advanced animals on earth. Today they are the most numerous and diverse group of vertebrates. There are approximately thirty thousand known species of fishes divided into four hundred families; there are more fishes than mammals, birds, reptiles, and amphibians combined.

From the Devonian period to the present, fishes have diver- **9**

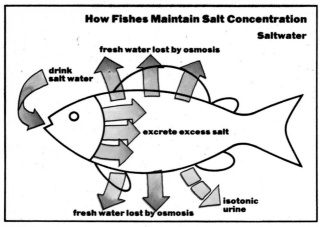

How Fishes Maintain Salt Concentration

Saltwater

fresh water lost by osmosis

drink salt water

excrete excess salt

fresh water lost by osmosis

isotonic urine

sified and now occupy nearly all the waters of the world, having successfully adapted to the highest alpine lakes and the abyssal depths of the sea. Members of the class Cephalaspidomorphi are the most primitive and include the hagfishes and lampreys. Their gills are contained in a series of separate muscular pouches, and their mouth is jawless. The sharks and rays, class Elasmobranchiomorphi, are more advanced and have jaws, individual gills with separate openings, and a cartilagenous skeleton. The bony fishes, class Teleostomi, constitute the largest group, encompassing all fishes with rayed fins.

Not only do fishes inhabit nearly all the waters of the world, they also occupy a wide variety of environmental niches and habitats. The bottoms of seas and lakes are covered not with plants, as the land is, but with a diverse group of organisms ranging from coral and mollusks to echinoderms and crustaceans. Fishes include herbivores that feed on aquatic plants and algae, grazers that feed on coral and other bottom-dwelling animals, and predators that feed on other fishes.

One feeding category that has no terrestrial counterpart is the plankton feeders. In the seas and fresh waters live minute and microscopic plants and animals known as phyto- and zooplankton. These organisms, which bloom and develop **10** massive concentrations, are the major food source for many

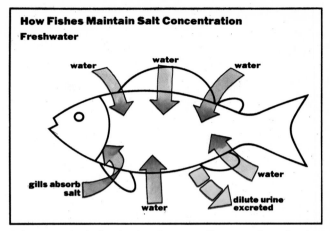

How Fishes Maintain Salt Concentration
Freshwater

water water water

gills absorb salt

water

water

dilute urine excreted

water

fishes, particularly the herrings, sardines, and anchovies. Plankton-feeding fishes have enormous gill rakers which act as sieves. As the fish swim through the productive areas, the plankton is strained from the water and swallowed. Even the largest animal ever to inhabit the earth, though not a fish but a mammal, the blue whale, has developed a method of straining plankton from the sea.

The physiological differences between salt and fresh water act as a barrier to fishes. Although some fishes do move back and forth between the two environments, total adaptation to both is rare. Freshwater fishes that live in the sea, such as salmon, return to fresh water to spawn; likewise, some gobies that live in fresh water return to the sea to spawn. A very few species are able to spawn in salt, fresh, or brackish water.

All fishes, whether fresh- or saltwater, have basically the same concentration of salt within their bodies: freshwater fishes are saltier than the water in which they live, and marine fishes are less salty. Specialized cells in the gills—salt-absorbing in freshwater fishes, salt-secreting in marine species—help maintain the equilibrium necessary to the fishes' survival.

Fishes are poikilothermic, or cold-blooded, animals, which means that their internal body temperature is dependent on **11** the environment. Compared with the terrestrial environment, the external thermal environment of fishes is much more stable, and many fishes cannot tolerate extreme temperature changes. Some species can live in captivity at temperatures significantly above or below their natural thermal optimum, but the physiological stresses they undergo as a result eventually cause them to become diseased or die.

Fishes have highly specialized sensory organs. Depending on the species, their vision ranges from acute to nonexistent. In some varieties, particularly those that live in murky water, vision is reinforced or even totally supplanted by electric organs that discharge impulses to detect changes in the environment.

Smell and taste are also vital senses in the underwater world. Specialized olfactory organs detect concentrations of odors in the magnitude of one part per billion. Many bottom-dwelling fishes have long chin whiskers or barbels that constantly probe the bottom, tasting everything in their search for food. Smell is also important to many fishes in migration and as a warning device. Injured minnows, for example, liberate a highly odorous substance from their skin that alerts other fishes to danger. Salmonids returning to their natal streams to spawn use odors to help them find their way.

Sound is more significant to underwater animals than it is to terrestrial vertebrates. Since underwater visibility is very poor, limited under the best conditions to less than four hundred feet, sound is extremely important in helping fishes to orient themselves, to locate food, even to maintain the integrity of schools. In addition to being an auditory organ, the fish's ear **12** also aids in maintaining equilibrium.

A part of the acoustical system that is unique to fishes is the lateral line, an elaborate system of specialized nerve cells distributed over the body surface. These nerves seem to detect low-frequency vibrations, alerting fish to the presence of other creatures around them. The system may be important for the maintenance of the integrity and movement of schools, and for the detection of prey or predators. In the aquarium, fishes sense the presence of the walls through the lateral line. Many blind or poorly sighted fishes show hyperdevelopment of this specialized nerve system.

The air bladder, a density-regulating mechanism located above the alimentary tract and slightly below the backbone, is not present in all fishes. The air bladder is basically a bubble of gas whose volume changes according to the depth of the water. By increasing the amount of air in the bubble, the fish increases its buoyancy, thus reducing the effort needed for swimming. Air bladders are of two types. The physostomous, or open-duct, type is connected to the alimentary canal by a tube, and the fish fills the bladder by gulping air at the water's surface. In the physoclistic, or closed-duct, type, no tube exists. Instead, a rete, or gas gland, secretes the gas—oxygen, nitrogen, or even carbon dioxide—into the bladder. The air bladder also has secondary functions. In some fishes it acts as a supplemental lung; in others it is connected to the ear and amplifies sounds and is sometimes used for sound production. Bottom-dwelling fishes frequently have no air bladders, whereas fishes that swim in mid-water or near the surface have the most developed.

It was probably the colors of fishes that first intrigued man and sparked his interest in maintaining them in captivity. **13**

Looking through the windows of a public aquarium or wandering through an aquarium store quickly reveals the wide variation in color of these creatures of the underwater world. It soon becomes apparent that the bright colors of birds are not unique and the ability to change colors is not confined to the chameleon.

One of the most important functions of color and color patterns is to provide camouflage for both prey and predator. Most fish that live near the surface, for example, are dark dorsally and silvery underneath. This adaptive countershading allows them to hide in the mirrorlike reflections of the surface waves. Flat fishes can take on the colors of their background and can sometimes match its texture as well. Camouflage is achieved by body shape as well as by color; many fish conceal themselves by appearing to be common objects in the environment. Among the best known are the leaf and angler fishes, which look like rocks and seaweed.

In addition to providing camouflage, color patterns afford protection in other ways. In many butterfly fishes, the eyes are covered by distinct bars, while the tail, which is shaped very much like the head, has a false eye spot. Predators, fooled by the arrangement, will attack the tail rather than the head, giving the butterfly fish a chance to dart away out of danger. Some poisonous relatives of the lion fish use color as a warning signal. Lying on the bottom, nearly concealed, they flash the bright colors on the undersides of their fins as a warning to possible predators. There is also mimicry in the sea: some serpent eels have color patterns that are very similar to venomous sea snakes.

14   Fishes, like other vertebrates, are sexual and possess male or

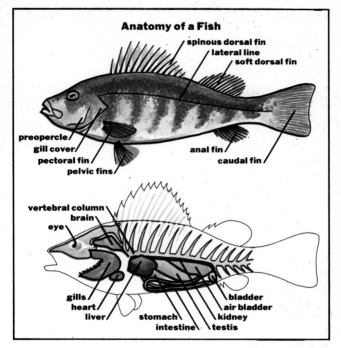

Anatomy of a Fish

spinous dorsal fin
lateral line
soft dorsal fin
preopercle
gill cover
pectoral fin
pelvic fins
anal fin
caudal fin

vertebral column
brain
eye
gills
heart
liver
stomach
intestine
bladder
air bladder
kidney
testis

female reproductive organs. In the majority of fishes fertilization is external. Spawning patterns range from elaborate nest building and parental care to simple scattering of eggs in which development is dependent on the environment. There are also live-bearing fishes, in which fertilization is internal. In many of these species the female can store the male's sperm, and a single mating may result in several broods.

Hermaphroditism has been observed among some fishes, particularly among the large family of sea basses and porgies. Hermaphroditic fish are not capable of self-fertilization, but in a single season an individual may play the role of both male and female, mother and father. Another unusual condition is sex reversal. In some species all fish are born of one sex and change roles with age. This again is most common in the sea bass family.

15

Fishes for the Aquarium

Of the nearly thirty thousand known species of fishes, only a few are suited for the aquarium environment. Generally, fishes from remote areas of the world and abyssal seas are not available. The physical requirements of other species make them unsuitable, and some have special social, physiological, or spatial criteria that must be met.

Like any other form of captive life, aquarium fishes depend on man and his attention for their survival, so providing the best possible care must be the home aquarist's uppermost goal. There are many decisions to be made before one fills a tank with water and introduces a live animal. The aquarist must select fishes that fit the size of the enclosure, provide an appropriate diet, and maintain a water quality suitable for the species. Fishes accustomed to living in hard, alkaline waters will not do well in soft water, and vice versa. For fishes that live in one environment and migrate to a totally different one to

Ryukin goldfish

spawn, reproduction in the aquarium may be impossible. The aquarist must learn as much as possible about his or her charges and be sensitive to their needs. Success is dependent on meeting the criteria established by the animal.

The size of the fishes selected is limited by the capacity of the aquarium and by the fishes' behavior, physiological requirements, and sociability. Large species are not ideal aquarium pets. They may be small enough as juveniles, but they will grow. Many people bring home what they think is a pretty little fish, then discover too late—perhaps after the disappearance of a number of favorite pets—that they have introduced a fast-growing predator into the tank.

Social behavior is one of the most important factors for the aquarist to consider. A definite social hierarchy will develop in the aquarium. It may be based on the size of the fishes, or on their aggressiveness or territorial requirements. Certain species are simply not compatible with one another, and spatial or territorial movements may not allow more than one fish of a kind in a particular aquarium. Fish that live in schools may exhibit abnormal behavior patterns, and in fact may not survive, if they are kept as individuals or in pairs. It is essential that the aquarist be aware of the fishes' community requirements before introducing new forms or even new individuals of the same species.

Knowledge of habits and habitats is also important in the selection process. The ideal community includes bottom-dwellers as well as fishes that swim near the surface, and solitary individuals as well as schooling fish. Bottom-dwellers should be selected that will be in view during the day and not always hiding or sleeping in a far corner. **17**

Maintaining the Aquarium

Fishes are living animals, and their survival depends on you. They require time and attention; occasionally they may even keep you at home or require a fish sitter. These obligations must be considered before any commitment is made to purchase a tank, its allied equipment, and its inhabitants. Careful thought can help prevent unnecessary disappointments and expense.

If you have never maintained fishes at home, it's best not to make any final decisions until you have gotten advice and opinions from the dealer and, if possible, from people who keep fishes or from the local aquarium hobbyist society. Too many aquariums are purchased on impulse, resulting in a disaster that ends with the fishes dead and the tank sitting on a shelf collecting dust and spiders.

One of your first and most important decisions will be whether you want freshwater or marine fishes. Marine fishes are popular because of the wide variety of species and their brilliant colors, but they are difficult to maintain. Sea water is the most stable physical environment in the world. Temperature fluctuations are negligible, and the water's chemical composition changes only minutely and at a slow rate. Bringing a piece of the ocean into your home or formulating it from synthetic ingredients affects the water's chemistry, salinity, pH, and ability to deal with waste products. Even a slight variation from the environment it is accustomed to can have adverse effects on a marine fish. In addition, because the equipment must be constructed of special materials, marine aquariums cost more; the fishes themselves are more expensive, too.

If you are truly a beginner, it may be best to start with a freshwater aquarium. Your initial investment will be lower, and, because freshwater fishes are more hardy and better able to tolerate slight imperfections and changes in water quality, your chances of losing fishes will be somewhat lower. Freshwater fishes, many of which are as colorful and attractive as
their marine counterparts, can be fascinating to maintain.

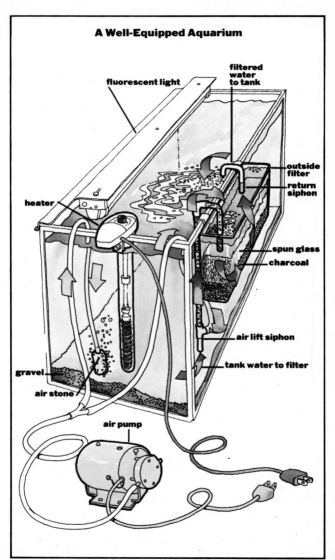

A Well-Equipped Aquarium

fluorescent light

filtered water to tank

outside filter

return siphon

heater

spun glass

charcoal

air lift siphon

tank water to filter

gravel

air stone

air pump

There is great satisfaction in reconstructing a natural environment in the home, watching the fishes begin a breeding cycle, and helping to create an ecologically balanced community.

Aquariums come in a multitude of sizes and shapes. The kind you select is a matter of individual taste, but as a general rule, it is wise to begin with as large a tank as is physically and economically feasible. For a marine aquarium, the tank should have at least a 30-gallon capacity, preferably more. The larger the tank, the easier it is to maintain the proper chemical balance.

Most tanks consist of a metal frame supporting glass sides, sealed with a waterproof caulking material. If you are considering a marine aquarium, however, you should look for a tank specifically designed to hold sea water. These are usually made either of acrylic plastic or of glass only, with no metal frame. Salt water has an extremely corrosive action on metal, which not only mars the appearance of the tank, but contributes toxins to the water.

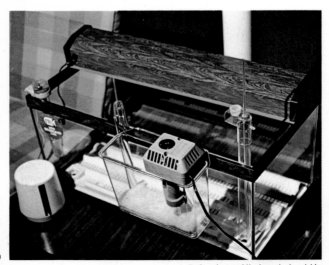

Before being filled, tank should be
outfitted with essentials such as air pump,
heater, and filter.

Water

Water is the external environment in which all fishes live, and as such it is the most important component of any aquarium. Water varies from one part of the country to another: it may be soft or hard, alkaline or acidic, filled with chemicals that give it a good or bad taste. The aquarist must always keep these variables in mind, for changes in water quality can cause fishes to go into shock or die. A fish should never be introduced into an aquarium without consideration of its previous environment.

An essential factor is the water's alkalinity or acidity. Because of the plant and animal debris dissolved in most lakes, rivers, and streams, fresh water is generally acid. Sea water, on the other hand, is more alkaline, because of the high concentration of salts. Acidity/alkalinity is measured on the pH scale, which runs from 0 (highest acid concentration) to 14 (highest alkaline concentration). Pure water, with a pH of 7, is neutral—neither acid nor alkaline. You can test the pH of the water in your tank with litmus paper, available in any pharmacy.

If you're setting up a freshwater aquarium, you may be tempted simply to fill the tank with water straight from the tap. But unless you live in a rural area and have access to well water, this isn't a good idea. Most tap water is treated with chlorine, and fishes' delicate gill membranes are extremely sensitive to this chemical. The simplest way to remove chlorine is to agitate the water overnight with an air stone or a diffuser, or to set it out in shallow trays in the sunlight for a few hours. There are also a number of effective chlorine-removing chemicals available.

The marine aquarist must decide whether to use natural or artificial sea water. Natural sea water is not necessarily the best choice. There is a good chance that it is contaminated with sewage and industrial wastes, and because it may be diluted by rivers pouring into it, water near the shore has a different composition from that bathing the coral reefs. If, despite these drawbacks, you do choose to use natural sea water, transport it **21** only in glass or plastic containers—never metal—and process it through a very fine filter before filling the tank. A better choice would be to use one of the many commercial salt mixes available. Though these formulas do not duplicate exactly the composition of natural sea water, they are safe and carry a far lower risk of pollution.

Once the tank is filled, the salinity of the water must be maintained at a stable level. Oceans, particularly in the tropics, generally have a salt concentration of 32–35 parts per thousand, a level that fluctuates very little except near the mouths of rivers. Too extreme or too rapid a change in salinity can kill a fish very quickly. Salinity itself is difficult to measure, but the density of water, which varies with salt concentration, can be measured with a simple hydrometer. A density of 1.025 roughly equals a salt concentration of 31 parts per thousand; a safe range for most marine fishes is a density between 1.019 and 1.026. pH should be between 8.0 and 8.3. Changes in pH or density can be caused by a multitude of factors, including overfeeding, accumulation of organic by-products of decay, or a build-up of carbon dioxide (the by-product of respiration). At the first sign of a change, the underlying cause should be determined and the problem corrected at once.

Keeping fishes in the home can and should be a pleasurable experience. There are three basic approaches to aquarium maintenance; most aquarists develop their own "wet-thumb" techniques, using elements of all three approaches. The simplest is the *natural* method, which requires aeration only and utilizes the plants and animals of the underwater environment to control wastes. This system supports relatively few fishes in a given volume of water, but it is quite rewarding to the aquarist who wants to create as natural an environment as possible. The *clinical,* or *sterile,* method employs high-rate filters, which literally scrub the water to provide as pure and clean an environment as mechanical and chemical techniques permit. Many aquarists prefer this method because it allows a fairly high concentration of fishes in any given unit of **22** water. The most common method is the *biological,* which acknowledges that there are beneficial bacteria in the environment that can convert organic waste products into nontoxic compounds.

Aeration and Filtration

Although fishes' metabolic processes are much slower than those of warm-blooded animals, their gills are constantly extracting dissolved oxygen from the water and simultaneously excreting carbon dioxide. To ensure an adequate oxygen supply, most aquarists use a small air pump and a diffusion or air stone in the tank. As air is pumped through the stone, small bubbles are created, which increase gas exchange.

Supplementary aeration is not always mandatory. It is possible to develop a balanced aquarium community in which the natural processes of photosynthesis and surface gas exchange provide sufficient oxygen. However, in order for these processes to take place, the tank must contain relatively few fishes. If a truly natural state is to exist, the population density within the tank must approximate that found in nature; the number of fishes per gallon of water in most streams, rivers, and oceans is very much lower than most people desire in an aquarium. Supplementary aeration not only adds oxygen to the water, it also circulates the water and aids in dissipating carbon dioxide, which might otherwise build up to toxic levels.

Filters function to remove wastes in aquariums in two ways. They help maintain visual clarity of the water by physically removing particles of excess food, feces, bacteria, and protozoa. In addition, filters aid in the removal of dissolved wastes or particles that are too small to be filtered physically. Filters and bottom sand collect bacteria which, through a process similar to digestion, break down potential toxins such as nitrites, ammonia, and proteins and render them harmless.

Filters take many forms, from simple air-powered plastic boxes set in a corner of the tank to elaborate mechanical devices that pump hundreds of gallons of water per minute. The size required depends on the size of the tank and the number of fishes it holds.

Lighting

Lighting is more than mere illumination. It has a direct effect on the diurnal and seasonal cycles of fishes and should be adjusted according to their needs. Tropical fishes live in zones of the world where the day-night ratio is nearly equal throughout the year, and aquarium fishes from these regions do well in a twelve-hour light-dark cycle. Temperate-zone fishes, on the other hand, require changes in the photoperiod (hours of exposure to light); in order to spawn, they need more light in the spring and less in the fall.

Since viewer pleasure is a factor in lighting arrangements, position must be considered. In most aquariums, the light source is located on top and toward the front, so that the fishes are illuminated and their colors highlighted. (If the light were positioned toward the rear of the tank, the fishes would be silhouetted.) Most aquarists prefer white light because it does not distort natural colors, but there are lights that create special effects for those who desire them.

High levels of light encourage plant growth, which may be beneficial or bothersome, depending on the ecology of the aquarium. Excessive light, including too much direct sunlight, should be avoided since it stimulates algae growth, which turns the water green and cloudy.

Heating

Nearly all aquarium fishes come from tropical regions, where the water temperature is a fairly constant 70°–85° F (21°–30° C). This range should be maintained in the home aquarium. Because this is warmer than the room temperature of the average home, supplemental heating is necessary.

A wide selection of heaters is available, from simple immersion types to more complex submersible varieties with built-in thermostats. The kind of heater you need depends on the room temperature and the size of the aquarium. Most heaters are equipped with instructions for computing thermal requirements. Thermostatically controlled heaters are recommended, **24** but a thermometer should always be installed so that you can tell at a glance if all is well. An aquarium heater should neither turn on and off frequently nor stay on continually. A heater that remains on may not have the capacity to maintain the desired temperature, particularly on a cold night. Although an oversize heater may sound like a good idea, it can be dangerous. Should the thermostat fail in the "on" position, the tank could be heated to a lethal temperature within a very short time.

Heaters should be placed near the filter or air stone so that the heated water is circulated evenly throughout the tank. And, because they can generate enough heat to crack the glass, they should never be placed in direct contact with the aquarium sides.

Decor

There are almost as many decorative materials available to the aquarist as there are fishes. In addition to artificial pottery and other ceramic knickknacks, natural items such as dead wood, rocks, and plants are attractive. The marine aquarist has all of the items available that freshwater aquarists have, except plants (algae—marine plants—are very difficult to grow, even for plant specialists and professionals) and has in addition shells, corals, sea fans, and live invertebrate animals such as anemones, tube worms, and shrimp.

Besides being visually pleasing, decorative items in the tank can help fulfill many of the biological requirements of the inhabitants. Some fishes need holes in which to hide; others, such as the damsel fishes of the coral reefs, like to cluster around particular types of coral. Certain kinds of bottom sand provide a place for wrasses to sleep, or for some flat fishes to demonstrate their ability to change color. Artificial and natural materials should be balanced, like the elements in a painting; correct composition makes an aquarium attractive.

Feeding

Like their terrestrial counterparts, fishes can be classified by their feeding habits as herbivores, carnivores, or omnivores. Fortunately for the aquarist, most fishes are omnivorous and **25** will eat both plant and animal matter. Many fishes that are primarily herbivorous in the wild will accommodate to a carnivorous diet in captivity. Some fish do have very specialized needs, and fish with bizarre appearances often have bizarre tastes, especially in the marine environment.

Perhaps the only general rule applicable to all fishes is to feed small amounts frequently. All excess food (except live food) will settle on the bottom and spoil, and decay is a far greater problem in the aquarium than underfeeding. The bacteria that feed on decaying material multiply extremely quickly, and since bacteria, like all living organisms, consume oxygen, a large bacterial bloom can literally suffocate the fishes. In addition, some bacteria liberate toxic substances and others cause disease.

Many prepared diets, such as dry flakes and pellets and freeze-dried worms and brine shrimp, are available for both freshwater and marine fishes, but they should not be used exclusively. Live food should be part of every fish's diet. In addition to being a treat for the fish, it provides essential trace elements. Live worms and brine shrimp are excellent supplements for marine species; the freshwater aquarist can choose from such organisms as daphnia, insect larvae, and infusoria, many of which can be collected from nearby ponds and streams. Live and chopped raw food should be rinsed thoroughly before it is placed in the aquarium, to remove excess body fluids that might promote bacterial growth; all food taken from natural sources should be examined carefully to ensure that the larvae of unwanted predators, such as dragonflies and water beetles, are not inadvertently introduced into the tank.

Marine fishes have more complex dietary requirements than freshwater fishes, but brine shrimp, chopped fish, and chopped shrimp are the staples for most species. For fishes that are algae or seaweed eaters, chopped spinach and lettuce can be good substitutes. Many marine fishes are browsers and grazers who feed continuously in their natural habitat; they **26** should be fed more frequently than others.

Problems and Disease

Whenever one keeps live animals, particularly wild or exotic pets, it is easier to avoid problems than to cure disease. When you set out to purchase a fish, make a special trip to the aquarium or pet shop; do not include it as part of your marketing. A fish may be perfectly healthy when it leaves the shop, but if it is left in its container for several hours on the front seat of an automobile, it may be excessively heated or cooled. By the time it is finally brought home, the fish will be thoroughly stressed and possibly unable to survive.

Most injuries and diseases result from improper handling. Anything that comes in contact with a fish, including your hands, must be immaculate. Use soaps and disinfectants to clean hands and equipment, but be sure to rinse them thoroughly, for any residue may be toxic to the fish. Extreme care should be taken in moving fishes, for their skin is very susceptible to injury. It is best to keep the fish in water while it is being moved—a plastic bag or a cup is preferable to a net. If a net must be used, it should be made of knotless material. If you have to touch a fish, make sure your hands are wet. If they are not, your fingers may stick to the fish's skin and pull off part of the delicate outer layer, leaving the fish vulnerable to disease and infection. Unlike terrestrial animals, fishes are constantly submerged in a bacteria-filled bath, and any abrasion or injury may allow pathogenic bacteria a foothold.

Disease can enter not only through injured skin but also through the sensitive mucous membranes of the gills and mouth. Gill diseases can be likened to the respiratory lung diseases of man.

Infectious diseases can be classified as parasitic, bacterial, viral, or fungal. Parasites may be brought into the home aquarium with a new fish or in contaminated water. In the wild, all fishes have parasites, but they exist in a proper balance and rarely cause death. In the artificial and crowded conditions of the aquarium, however, parasites' life cycles may be accelerated, resulting in higher exposure rates for the fishes. Acute infestations of parasites debilitate the fishes and **27** can be lethal; parasitism is one of the major causes of death in marine species. The usual symptoms of parasitic disease—marked changes in the fishes' behavior and breathing rates and an unwillingness to eat—are fairly easy to recognize. Treatment generally consists of administering chemicals that kill the parasites.

"White spot" is one of the most common parasitic diseases to attack aquarium fishes. A protozoan (single-cell animal) known as *Cryptocaryon* causes the disease in marine species; in fresh water the protozoan responsible is the well-known *Ichthyophthirius* ("ich"). Infested fish show labored breathing, and their bodies become covered with white spots as if sprinkled with salt. Bathing the fishes in quinine, acriflavin, and copper sulfate usually destroys the protozoa.

Bacterial diseases often affect fishes that have been injured. The most frequent signs of bacterial infections are lesions and deteriorating fins; the most effective treatments are antibiotics (particularly chlormycetin, bacitracin, penicillin, and acriflavin), used either in the aquarium itself or in separate baths.

The most common viral disease, in both fresh and salt water,

Long-nose butterfly fish with lymphocystis. Note white nodules on fins and body.

is lymphocystis, which can be recognized by the white nodules that appear on the fish's fins and body. Because this disease is often associated with stress, poor water quality, and overcrowding, proper aquarium management is the best prevention and cure. Viruses do not respond to antibiotics, so fishes with this disease must be isolated to prevent further spread.

Fungal diseases are among the most difficult to diagnose, but are relatively simple to cure. Outbreaks can be controlled with such chemicals as malachite green and with preparations intended for ringworm in humans.

In a well-kept aquarium, new diseases should not appear every day, but they are always a possibility. Poor water quality, improperly regulated temperatures, overcrowding, and incorrect diet can all contribute to stress, which in turn lowers resistance to disease. Every aquarist should have one of the many excellent books outlining the most common diseases of aquarium fishes and should have on hand some of the common remedies.

29

Top: Swordtail with melanoma, a pigmented tumor at the base of its tail. Bottom: Guppy with "white spot" or "ich," one of the more common parasitic diseases.

Aquarium Fishes

Fishes are classified according to their relationships, not according to environmental requirements. Dividing fishes into marine and freshwater categories would lead to duplication, for although most fishes live predominantly in one environment or the other, members of the same family cross the boundary between them. The classification system used by ichthyologists is based on the phylogenetic viewpoint, which suggests a scheme leading from the historically oldest and least specialized to the most advanced or specialized fishes.

Elasmobranchiomorphi: Sharks, Skates, and Rays

Sharks, skates, and rays are included in a single zoological class because they all have cartilagenous skeletons and share a similar jaw structure. In addition, the sharks and rays have distinctive scales called denticles (literally, "little teeth"), which are similar in structure to and have the same embryological origin as their teeth.

This class includes both live bearers and egg layers; fertilization is internal in all species. Males are easily differentiated from females by the presence of claspers, fleshy reproductive organs attached to the pelvic fins.

None of the Elasmobranchiomorphi have air bladders, and very few species enter fresh water. They are difficult fishes to maintain in captivity. Their large size makes them poorly suited for aquarium life, and the lack of a bony skeleton makes them difficult to transport without injury.

Selachii: Sharks

Sharks are among the most easily and universally recognized fishes in the world. There are approximately 250 known species. The most notorious family is the mackerel sharks, Isuridae, which includes the great white shark (Carcharodon carcharias) and the mako shark (Isurus glaucus). The requiem family (Carcharhinidae) also includes many large and dangerous species. Very few members of these families have been

maintained in captivity, and no great white shark has ever lived in even the largest public aquarium. The largest sharks are the basking *(Cetorhinus maximus)* and whale sharks *(Rhincodon typus)* which exceed forty feet (12 m) in length. Unlike mackerel and requiem sharks, basking and whale sharks are plankton-feeders and not dangerous to humans.

Only a few shark species are suitable for aquariums, and of these only juveniles are maintained successfully.

Nurse Shark *(Ginglymostoma cirratum)*
Family Orectolobidae

These large bottom-dwelling sharks are easily recognized by their two dorsal fins and the short barbels, or whiskers, extending from each nostril. Nurse sharks are less than two feet long (61 cm) at birth, and individuals have been maintained successfully in home aquariums for several years before outgrowing their tanks. Adults may grow to fourteen feet (4 m). Although, like all sharks, they are capable of inflicting serious wounds, nurse sharks are not considered dangerous.

Nurse sharks are found in the tropical and subtropical Atlantic Ocean and in the tropical eastern Pacific, most commonly around coral reefs and rocky outcrops. They feed on fish and invertebrates in the wild; in the aquarium they readily accept small pieces of fish, clams, and shrimps. **31**

Nurse shark

California Swell Shark *(Cephaloscyllium uter)*
Family Scyliorhinidae

This family, popularly known as cat sharks, has representatives in all the seas of the world. There are a few deep-sea species, but most cat sharks live close to the shore. They are generally less than three feet (9 m) long, and the deep-sea species include the smallest sharks in the world.

Swell sharks are distinguished by their compressed body, their two dorsal fins, and their mottled coloration. They inhabit rocky reefs in the Pacific from central California to Chile. Nocturnal feeders, they often hide deep within rocky crevices during the day. When excited or threatened, they defend themselves by swallowing large quantities of water and inflating the body so that they cannot be extracted from the crevice.

32   Swell sharks are egg layers. Mating occurs in the spring, and

"Mermaid's purse," California swell shark embryo in egg case

the females store the sperm deposited by the males for at least eight months. During the egg-laying season, the eggs are fertilized as they pass through the oviducts. Once they are laid, the eggs, rectangular with coiled tendrils extending from each corner, attach themselves to seaweed, rocks, and sea fans at the ocean bottom. These eggs, sometimes called "mermaids' purses," can be found along the sea bottom through most of the summer, and it is possible to maintain the developing embryo in the aquarium. After a seven- to nine-month incubation period, the young shark is hatched. The newborn is well developed, with the appearance of an adult. Feeding may not begin for several days or weeks after hatching.

Swell sharks are carnivorous scavengers and, like many other bottom-dwelling fishes, have varied feeding habits. They accept cut fish, shrimps, clams, mussels, and lobsters. **33**

California swell shark

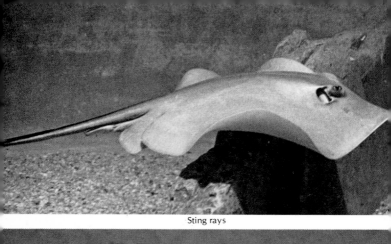

Sting rays

Raiiformes: Rays

Rays are easily recognized by their flat bodies and enlarged pectoral fins. Most rays are marine, but the group also includes freshwater rays and sawfishes.

Most rays are bottom-dwellers, with their mouths and gills located on the underside of the body, so it is virtually impossible for them to breathe through their mouths. Many species, therefore, have developed an unusual method of respiration: water is taken in through the spiracle, an opening at the top of the head, and is passed over the gills and expelled through the underside gill slits.

There are about 340 known species of rays. They range in size from fish only a few inches in diameter to the large mantas, which may measure twenty feet (6 m) from fin tip to fin tip. As would be expected in such a diverse group, their feeding habits range from digging mollusks to feeding on plankton.

Rays are extremely difficult to maintain in captivity, but a few freshwater sting rays are available for the home aquarium.

Sting Ray (Dasyatis sp.)
Family Dasyatidae

All of the 118 species in this family have a slender, tapered, grooved spine located at the base of the tail and associated with a poison gland. When a sting ray attacks its prey, the grooves in the spine guide a lethal poison from the gland into the inflicted wound. A sting ray's spine, like a shark's teeth, will regenerate if it is removed.

Sting rays inhabit shallow waters in the tropics, where they are quite common. Many people wading near the shore at tropical beaches have been severely injured by sting rays—their teeth are capable of cracking even the toughest clam shells.

Sting rays range in size from one and a half pounds and a few inches across to more than 750 pounds (340 kg) and six to seven feet (1.8–2 m) across. Reproduction occurs by internal fertilization, and the young are born alive. In the aquarium sting rays do best on live food: fish, clams, mussels, or shrimp. **35**

Teleostomi: Bony Fishes

The bony fishes are the most diverse and abundant vertebrates in the world; representatives are found in every inhabitable waterway.

The bony fishes differ from the sharks, skates, and rays in having, as their name implies, a skeleton made up of calcified bones. The internal gills are similar in function and appearance to those of the Elasmobranchiomorphi, but they do not have separate openings to the exterior. Instead, they are covered by a single gill plate, called the operculum, and only one opening exists. Fins are generally composed of bony spines or rays connected to one another by membranes.

Most Teleostomi are egg layers, although there are some live bearers found in both fresh and salt water. Copulation is accomplished by a specialized anal fin in the male that permits internal fertilization. Most bony fishes have an air bladder, although certain species that live on or near the bottom lack this organ. With the exception of a few families, nearly all bony fishes are covered with scales.

The Teleostomi are subdivided into three main groups: the lungfishes, or Dipnoi; the fringe fins, or Crossopteryigii, which include the ancient coelacanth; and the ray fins, or Actinopterigii, which are the most abundant and are the fishes for aquariums.

Polypteriformes: Polypterids

The polypterids can be distinguished from all other spiny ray fishes by their distinctive dorsal fin: instead of a single fin they have five to eight flaglike finlets, each bony ray being branched. The polypterids also have a distinctive fan-shaped pectoral that contains a fleshy lobe with scales. Although the caudal fin appears to be symmetrical, it is actually heterocercal, the vertebral column running into the upper lobe. These characteristics, plus the existence of a spiral fold in the intestine, are considered primitive, indicating that the group is
indeed very old.

Bichir *(Polypterus weeksi)*

Family Polypteridae

Bichirs, members of a primitive family related to the fringe fins, are found in the fresh waters of Africa. The name *Polypterus*, which means "many fins," suits them well. Their dorsal fin appears to be a single structure, but it is actually made up of many separate finlets, and each fin spine has several branching rays. Bichirs are born with frilled external gills, which they lose by the time they reach adulthood.

The bichirs' air bladder functions as an auxiliary lung. If they cannot get to the surface to breathe, bichirs will die of suffocation. They have a remnant spiracle and a digestive tract that includes a spiral valve, features they share with the sharks, rays, lungfishes, and coelacanths.

Little is known of the bichirs' breeding habits except that they leave their rivers and lakes during the rainy season (from June to September) to lay their eggs in the dense plant life of the swamps. Because they are highly predatory, bichirs are not usually kept in aquariums.

37

Bichir

Lepisosteiformes: Gars

Gars have elongated bodies with an armorlike covering of diamond-shaped scales. These two-layered scales are close-set but do not overlap. Their hard surface gives the appearance of polished ivory. The head is protected by bony plates, and the protruding jaws look like an alligator's snout. Gars have dorsal and anal fins only, which are located to the rear of the body. The caudal fin is heterocercal. As with bichirs, the intestinal spiral valve indicates that they are primitive fishes. There are about ten species in North and Central America and Cuba, most of which are freshwater inhabitants.

Long-nosed Gar *(Lepisosteus osseus)*

Family Lepisosteidae

Gars, native to North America, are found in the waters of the eastern United States from Vermont to Mississippi. The largest member of the family is the alligator gar, which reaches a
38 length of ten feet (3 m).

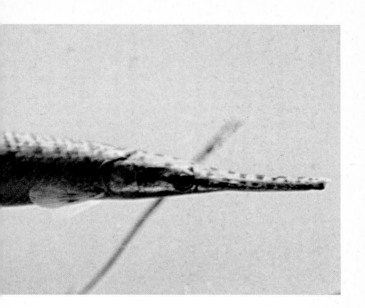

Like the bichirs and other primitive fishes, gars must have access to the surface in order to breathe, and they use the air bladder as an auxiliary respiratory organ. The air bladder also allows them to remain out of water for as long as twenty-four hours. When being transported, they may simply be kept wet and covered.

The long-nose is the most colorful gar species and the one best suited for aquarium life. It will reach a length of four feet (1.2 m), but its growth rate is slow, and long-nosed gars have been maintained for more than twenty years in captivity.

The long-nose's jaws account for more than 75 percent of its total head length, giving the species the snoutlike appearance from which it takes its name. The needlelike teeth snap and seize small fishes with a sideways thrust of the head similar to that of the crocodilian reptiles.

Long-nosed gars are found in fresh water throughout the northeastern United States. Their typical habitat is shallow, slow-moving rivers and ponds.

39

Long-nosed gar

Anguilliformes: Eels

Eels are distinguished from almost all other fishes by their long, snakelike bodies. The body is generally cylindrical, but some marine morays are compressed laterally and have a more typically fishlike appearance. Eels have no spiny rays in their fins, and they lack ventral fins entirely. Some species also lack a caudal fin, or tail. Many eels are scaleless; if scales are present, they are very small. The air bladder may or may not be well developed; it is connected by an opening to the foregut. The simile "as slippery as an eel" is quite accurate, for all eels secrete copious amounts of mucus, which makes their skin quite slimy.

All eels are marine. Adult European and American eels live in fresh water, but they return to the sea to spawn. The adult eels, after leaving the rivers of Europe and America, swim to the central Atlantic in the region of the Sargasso Sea to spawn. After hatching, the larvae drift with the currents; by the time they reach the coasts of North America and Europe, they have metamorphosed into elvers.

In addition to the "freshwater" eels, the order includes the marine morays, the congers, and the snake, garden, and deepwater eels. Only a few species are suitable for aquariums, and of these, young morays are most readily available.

Leaf-nosed Moray *(Rhinomuraena ambionensis)*
Family Muraenidae

Although the leaf-nosed morays of the Indo-Pacific region are extremely difficult to maintain in captivity, they are sought after by marine aquarists because of their striking and colorful appearance. All morays have a keen sense of smell, which helps them to locate food. In the leaf-nosed morays the forward tubular nostril has an accentuated leaflike structure. They have sharp teeth, including large canines located in the roof of the mouth, and feed on small invertebrates of the coral reef. Because of this specialized diet, only aquarists with an available source of small live shrimp should attempt to maintain these morays.

40

Leaf-nosed moray ▶

Most morays are innocuous creatures, hiding during the day in the deep recesses of rocky and coral reefs. Because of their poor eyesight and dependence on olfaction, they often come out to investigate activity. Their unusual manner of breathing (they ingest water through their mouth by a pumping action, then expel it through the small round gill openings) makes them appear to be constantly biting, which may account for the abundance of myths about morays. They are considered by some to be the "rattlesnakes of the sea," and nearly every deep-sea diver has stories about a spine-tingling encounter with a moray. Not all these stories are exaggerations. The larger species reach lengths of at least nine feet (3 m), and their powerful canines are capable of inflicting serious wounds. Some morays have poison glands associated with their canines, and their bite is more painful than a simple laceration.

Zebra Moray *(Echidna zebra)*

Family Muraenidae

This strikingly beautiful black-and-white-barred species inhabits the tropical Indo-Pacific region. Its body is thicker than that of most eels—it may grow to twelve inches (30.5 cm) from back to belly, and four and a half feet (1.4 m) in length.

The zebra moray is one of the more suitable species for home aquariums. It is not as voracious as other members of the family, and it does not prey on other fishes. Its small pebblelike teeth are suitable for crushing shells, and it feeds mainly on invertebrates, worms, and shellfish. The aquarist should be prepared to supply it with live shrimp rather than prepared foods. Because zebra morays are nocturnal, they should be fed in the early evening or when the tank is dark.

Like all other eels, the zebra moray is a bottom-dweller and will remain hidden most of the time. In a well-decorated aquarium, however, parts of its body can always be seen. It is a passive species, and its movements around the bottom of the aquarium will not damage the decor or harm the other fishes.

Zebra moray ▲ Arowana ▶

Osteoglossiformes: Bony Tongues

This order of freshwater fishes includes the arowanas, butterfly fishes, and featherfins. These fishes have long bodies covered with large scales, and long dorsal and anal fins. All Osteoglossiformes are predatory, and their bony, tooth-covered tongues, from which the order takes its name, are used to capture prey.

Arowana *(Osteoglossum bicirrhosum)*
Family Osteoglossidae

The family Osteoglossidae, found in South America, Africa, Malaysia, and Australia, contains only six species. One of them, the Amazonian arapaima *(Arapaima gigas)*, is one of the world's largest freshwater fishes.

The arowana, which inhabits the Amazon River basin, is easily recognized by the two barbels located at the tip of the lower jaw, by its large 45-degree-angled mouth, and by its bright silver color and large scales which reflect rainbowlike colors.

Arowanas prefer open waters and generally swim close to the surface. In the wild, they feed on fish and freshwater

shrimp. In captivity, they readily accept any small living fish or shrimp, and adults are able to swallow larger specimens.

Reproduction takes place in shallow weedy areas. After they have been spawned and fertilized externally, the eggs are brooded ten to twenty days in the female's mouth, in a pouch located between the lower jaws.

Arowanas may reach a length of two feet (61 cm). Although they are not ideal aquarium species, many people maintain them because of their spectacular silver color and their ability to live in a relatively small container. Because they are jumpers, their tank must be kept covered at all times.

▲ Butterfly fish ▼ Featherfin

Butterfly Fish *(Pantodon buckholzi)*

Family Pantodontidae

This small freshwater fish of the African Niger and Congo rivers is the only species in the family Pantodontidae. Unlike most Osteoglossiformes, it is not large and does not have large scales. This species is not related to the marine butterfly fishes, which obtain their name from their bright colors and resemblance to butterflies. *Pantodon buckholzi* was named for the naturalist Buckholz, who first observed it in the wild and brought back tales of a fish that could "fly." Actually, the butterfly fish does not fly, it leaps. In the aquarium, precautions must be taken to keep it from jumping out of the tank.

The unusually large pectoral fins enable the species to hang suspended beneath the surface and help it glide when jumping. The long threadlike rays of the pelvic fins are tactile receptors and aid the fish in locating the flying insects and insect larvae that make up the bulk of its diet. In the aquarium, the butterfly fish readily accepts mealworms and other foods that float or sink slowly.

Pantodon has been successfully bred in captivity. After spawning, the sticky eggs float and attach themselves to plants. Because of its tropical origin, the butterfly fish does best in water temperatures of 74°–80° F (23°–27° C).

Featherfin *(Notopterus chitala)*

Family Notopteridae

All members of this family have long, compressed, tapered bodies which reach lengths of up to two feet (61 cm). The anal fin begins under the head and continues along the underside of the body, finally merging with the caudal fin. There is also, in the middle of the back, a delicate, featherlike dorsal fin with six or seven rays—hence the name featherfin.

Featherfins live in quiet and sometimes stagnant waters and prefer warm tropical temperatures between 75° and 80° F (24°–27° C). Their air bladder functions as a lung. They will accept nearly any type of food, but large specimens are predators and not ideal for the communal aquarium. **45**

Mormyriformes: Mormyrids

The mormyrids are a relatively large group (110 species) inhabiting tropical Asia and Africa. Most are solitary bottom-dwellers, but there are a few species that school. Their diet consists mainly of bottom-dwelling organisms such as worms, shrimp, and insect larvae.

Mormyrids' bodies are generally compressed and dark-colored, and the body narrows dramatically in front of the forked tail. Their dorsal and anal fins are opposite one another and set far back on the body. The mouth is typically located on the underside of the head and, depending on the species, may be associated with a variety of unusual forms such as an elephantlike nose or projecting lower lips or jaws.

The most striking feature of this order, however, is not visible. Mormyrids have the largest brains of any fishes, and they produce and utilize electrical charges.

It is well known that electric eels, catfishes, and torpedo rays discharge electricity as a defense mechanism and use large currents to stun and capture prey. Mormyrids, however, utilize electricity as a sensory device, to detect environmental changes and the presence of prey or predators. They discharge

a relatively weak current and can detect variations in the field as small as .000003 amperes. They have four internal electric organs, which together make up nearly one-fifth their total body length. These organs are modified muscle cells which generate electric current. In addition, specialized cells in the skin and lateral line detect minute amounts of electrical current, enabling mormyrids to sense the approach of other fishes or objects.

Ubangi Mormyrid *(Gnathonemus petersi)*
Family Mormyridae

This fish is distinguished by its long, protruding lower lip, which it uses to locate food. In a five-inch-long fish the lower lip may protrude one-half inch, or nearly 10 percent of the total body length.

The Ubangi mormyrid is a native of the slow-moving and stagnant waters of the Congo River in Africa and appears to prefer temperatures between 72° and 86° F (22°–30° C). It is considered to be anadromous (migratory), since it leaves the slow-moving lakes and swamps to spawn in rivers. Males are differentiated from females by the concave shape and longer rays of their anal fin.

47

Ubangi mormyrid

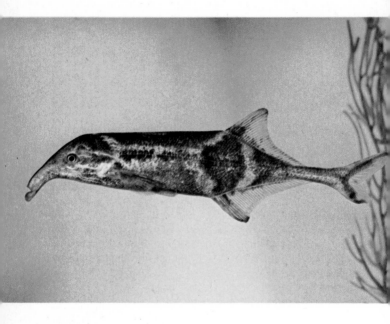

Elephant-nosed Mormyrid *(Gnathonemus tamandua)*

Family Mormyridae

As their common name indicates, elephant-noses are among the more bizarre-looking members of the family Mormyridae. The elongated trunk, with the mouth, makes up nearly a quarter of the total body length. The small mouth contains only a few teeth. The tip of the trunk acts as a sensory organ adapted for touching and tasting the environment.

The elephant-nose is a bottom-feeder and will probe the bottom and crevices to find insect larvae, shrimp, and other suitable food organisms. Native to the upper Nile, the elephant-nose prefers water temperatures between 72° and **48** 82° F (22°–28° C).

Elephant-nosed mormyrid

Cypriniformes: Characins, Electric Fishes, and Carps

The characins, electric fishes, and carps, and their distant relatives the catfishes, belong to a superorder known as Ostariophysi. Together they comprise six thousand species of freshwater fishes distributed throughout the world exclusive of Australia and Antarctica. The one feature they all have in common is an internal anatomical structure known as the webbarian apparatus, a series of tiny bones that link the air bladder to the inner ear. These bones, analogous to the auditory ossicles of mammals, are necessary for hearing and are not to be confused with the otoliths, which are essential for equilibrium. The webbarian bones serve as conductors for the ear, and the air bladder receives and amplifies sounds.

Because of this specialized apparatus, many Ostariophysi are extremely sensitive to sound. In some characins the sensitivity is heightened because the air bladder is located near the surface of the skin and may serve as an "eardrum." Many carps emit high-frequency sounds by vibrating the air bladder or forcing air through the duct that connects the air bladder to the throat. It is believed that some Ostariophysi use echolocation similar to the "sonar system" of bats and dolphins. By sending out high-frequency sounds and listening to the returning echoes, animals can detect and identify prey, predators, and the limits of their environment.

The superorder Ostariophysi contains two orders: Cypriniformes, which includes the characins, electric fishes, and carps; and Siluriformes, the catfishes. Because of the great diversity among its members, the order Cypriniformes has been further broken down into three suborders: Characoidei, the characins; Gymnotoidei, the electric fishes; and Cyprinoidei, the minnows, barbs, and carps. In most Cypriniformes, the pelvic fins are attached near the center of the abdomen, and there is a single dorsal fin. In some carps the dorsal fin is preceded by a large fused ray. The characins frequently have a fatty, rayless adipose fin between the dorsal and caudal fins.

Characoidei: Characins

The fifteen hundred species of characins are limited to the fresh waters of tropical and subtropical America and Africa. In tropical America, which has more freshwater fishes than any other part of the world, nearly half of all the freshwater species are characins.

Characins exhibit wide diversity in body form and habits. They range from less than one inch (2.5 cm) to more than five feet (1.5 m) in length, and include vegetarians, carnivores, and omnivores. Of the carnivores, the best known are the South American piranhas and the African tiger fish, both dangerous to man. The African tiger fish, which may weigh up to 125 pounds (57 kg), is dangerous as an individual; piranhas attack in large schools, and any animal may be prey to them.

Bloodfins (Aphyocharax rubripinnis)
Family Characidae

Because of their attractive appearance and relatively simple needs, these slender, 2¼-inch-long (6-cm), minnowlike fishes of the Piranha River and the Rio de la Plata have become popular aquarium fishes. They live at lower temperatures than most tropical fishes and will survive in captivity at temperatures above 68° F (20° C). They prefer soft water with a neutral pH.

Bloodfins

Bloodfins are among the more colorful inhabitants of the underwater world. They take their name from their striking, bright red fins. Their metallic blue-and-silver body reflects hues varying from green to yellow, depending on the light, and they have a green spot on the gill cover. Bloodfins breed in shallow water. The sexes are differentiated slightly in that the females are somewhat larger than the males.

Because they are schooling fish and live in open waters, bloodfins do best in sparsely planted aquariums. However, they do need some aquatic plants for protection during breeding. They eat plankton in the wild, but do well on prepared commercial foods in captivity.

Disc characin

Disc Characin (*Ephippicharax orbicularis*)

Family Characidae

The disc characin, the only member of its genus, is widely distributed in the Amazon drainage basin in Peru, Brazil, and the Guianas. It prefers open waters, although it generally remains near areas where plants are available for hiding. *Ephippicharax* typically is under four inches (10 cm) long, though some individuals grow to almost six inches. The body is compressed laterally and nearly disclike in shape, hence the common name. The scales are bright silver and change subtly in hue with the lighting. The back of the fish may range from olive-green to brown, and the males have an intense black stripe on the anterior edge of the anal fin.

Although lively and mobile, this species does well in the aquarium. Little is known of its reproductive patterns in the wild, but it has been bred successfully in captivity. Like many other characins, it is a schooling fish and does best when it is kept with other members of its species. When two or more disc characins are together, for reasons unknown, they frequently do a peculiar bobbing dance, beating the pectoral fins in unison as they hang nearly motionless in the water.

Glowlight Tetra (*Hemigrammus erythrozonus*)

Family Characidae

Within the family Characidae there is a large subgroup of fishes commonly known as tetras. They comprise between forty and forty-five genera, some of which contain more than fifty species each. Among these are the genera *Astyanax, Moenkhausia, Hyphessobrycon,* and *Hemigrammus,* which together account for the vast majority of South American tetras imported into the United States.

Tetras feed primarily on small insects and larvae, as well as most plant matter. Because they are quite easy to maintain, they are favorites with beginning aquarists.

The glowlight tetra is undoubtedly one of the more popular species. Its basically greenish body is divided horizontally on each side by an iridescent fiery red stripe that extends from the caudal fin to the top of the eye. The dorsal and anal fins are pink, and the pelvic fins may be tipped with white or ice-blue. Adults reach a length of one and a half inches (4 cm).

Glowlights are peaceful schooling fishes native to the Guianas and the lower Amazon basin. They prefer slightly acid water, with a pH just below 7. Easily bred in captivity, the species will spawn almost spontaneously. To ensure successful spawning, the aquarist should see that the tank contains a number of fine-leafed plants. The glowlight's eggs, like those of many other tetras, are slightly adhesive, and, though some sink to the bottom and wedge between pebbles, many stick to the plants; these have the best chance of survival. Even the eggs that fall to the bottom, however, should not all die. If the temperature is maintained between 68° and 79° F (20°–26° C), the young should be hatched within a few days.

Glowlight tetras. Female (above) is slightly larger and rounder.

Head-and-Tail-Light Tetra *(Hemigrammus ocellifer)*

Family Characidae

Head-and-tail-light tetras come from the same regions as the glowlight. Peaceful fish, they are particularly attractive aquarium specimens because of their coloration: they are gleaming silver with dark-edged scales, and they have a deep black spot at the base of the caudal fin, topped by a splash of iridescent red. This is the "tail light" of the species' common name; the "head light" is a similar iridescent patch above the eyes.

There is greater differentiation between male and female in this species than there is in many other tetras. The female's body is broader and deeper than the male's, and most males have a distinctive stripe on the anal fin. Adults of both sexes reach a length of almost two inches (5 cm).

Head-and-tail-lights prefer a temperature range of 64°–82° F (18°–28° C) and thick plant growth in the aquarium. They are relatively easy to breed. The eggs either attach themselves to bushy plants or settle on the pebbly aquarium bottom and usually hatch within three days.

54

Head-and-tail-light tetra ▲ Diamond tetra ▶

Diamond Tetra *(Moenkhausia pittieri)*

Family Characidae

Diamond tetras are natives of Venezuela and are particularly abundant in Lake Valencia. This species is distinguished by its straight lateral line and laterally compressed body. Its color ranges from silvery gray to soft green, and the scales are quite apparent. In the aquarium, light shining on the scales produces a bright, sparkling effect that gives the diamond tetra its name. The species has extremely large fins, with the dorsal and anal fins enlarged in the males.

Diamond tetras should be maintained in a roomy aquarium with a temperature of about 75° F (24° C). Diamond tetras have been common in aquariums since 1933 and breed well in captivity. Several hundred eggs are laid at each spawning and incubate for about three and a half days. After hatching, the young hang onto plants and the aquarium walls for two days or so before they begin swimming and feeding on infusoria.

Rosy Tetra *(Hyphessobrycon bentosi)*
Family Characidae

This attractive species is native to the Guianas and the lower Amazon basin. It reaches a length of about two inches (5 cm) and is distinguished by its rosy pink body, short snout, and upturned mouth. The anal and ventral fins and the margin of the caudal fin are bright red, the first rays of the anal and dorsal fins are white-tipped, and the upper half of the dorsal fins is deep black.

The rosy tetra is a peaceful but lively fish. It is recommended that it be maintained in the aquarium at least in pairs. Adult males are distinguished by their long, high dorsal fin and a long ray on the anterior portion of the anal fin. During courtship the males do a distinctive dance around the females. Once the mate is selected the male swims about—left and right, up and down—showing off his sparkling colors. The dance ends with both parents shaking their bodies together. Once all the eggs are laid and settle to the bottom they hatch within about three days. The juveniles eat infusoria for the first **56** week, then switch to live baby brine shrimp.

Rosy tetra ▲ Mexican tetras ▶

Mexican Tetra *(Astyanax fasciatus)*

Family Characidae

Astyanax is the most widely distributed characin genus—it ranges from Argentina to southern North America. Because of their relatively plain appearance and shape, members of this genus are not among the favorite fishes of home aquarists.

The species *Astyanax fasciatus*, distributed throughout Central America and Mexico, includes several blind varieties. These cave-dwelling fishes are so different from their above-ground relatives that for a number of years they were placed in a separate genus, *Anoptichthys* (literally, "fish without eyes"). The blind varieties lack pigmentation, and their body appears pinkish white. In spite of the great differences between the river fishes with normal vision and the blind cave fishes, the varieties can be crossbred, producing completely fertile hybrid offspring.

Cardinal Tetra *(Cheirodon axelrodi)*

Family Characidae

The cardinal tetra is probably the most widely known tetra. It is closely allied with the neon tetra, which has recently been reclassified in a new genus, *Paracheirodon*. Both neon and cardinal tetras are distinguished by a brilliant neon-blue horizontal stripe, set off by a red stripe immediately below it. In the cardinal tetra, the red band extends forward to the head, whereas in the neon it stops near the base of the anal fin.

Cardinal tetras, native to Brazil and Colombia, require soft, somewhat acidic water, with a pH ranging from 4.5 to 6.8, and bushy plants in which to scatter their adhesive eggs. Sexual differentiation is apparent only near spawning time, when the females become enlarged with the eggs they are carrying.

Cardinal tetra

Neon Tetra *(Paracheirodon innesi)*
Family Characidae

Although similar in many ways to the cardinal tetra, this popular beginner's fish has been placed in a separate genus. Neon tetras have two rows of teeth in the jaws, whereas cardinal tetras have a single row. Both species inhabit similar environments and have evolved similar or parallel appearances. Apparently, the brilliant neon aids species recognition in the dark river water of the Amazon.

The neon tetra has been known to home aquarists perhaps longer than any other member of the tetra group, and it still retains its popularity. Its breeding habits are similar to other tetras. Aquarium temperatures must never be more than 68–72° F (20–22° C), and the pH 6.2–6.8.

To best appreciate the glowing colors of neon tetras the aquarist should see that the tank is neither too bright nor overly stocked with plants. In the dark environment of the aquarium, the neon bands appear to glow at their best in near twilight. **59**

Neon tetras

Piranha *(Serrasalmus nattereri)*
Family Characidae

Piranhas are perhaps the most feared and least understood of the bony fishes. Their strong jaws and extremely sharp, serrated teeth enable them to bite through flesh and small bones, and there are innumerable stories told of travelers unwittingly entering piranha-filled waters and being quickly devoured. Many of these tales, however, are exaggerated. Undoubtedly piranhas are dangerous—to man and to any animal that enters their environment—but not every encounter results in an attack. Although attacks have been reported and natives can show you evidence of piranha bites, there are very few documented accounts of humans actually being killed by piranhas. Piranhas are primarily fish eaters, and they are group predators. A single eight-to-ten-inch (20–25-cm) piranha is incapable of an attack that will kill a person or a large beast. However, they can inflict serious wounds, and a group will

attack if it scents blood. These fish should be approached and handled only with extreme caution.

Piranhas are distinguished from other characins primarily by their jaw structure and dentition. Depending on the ichthyological text consulted, there are between a dozen and three dozen piranha species, some of which are more voracious than others. The red piranha, *Serrasalmus nattereri*, which lives near the mouth of the Amazon, is considered one of the most dangerous.

Unlike other characins, piranhas care for their eggs during the incubation period. As many as five thousand adhesive eggs may be spawned and fertilized at one time. The eggs attach themselves to underwater plants, and the male guards the nest for ten to eighteen days until they hatch.

In the United States, importation of piranhas is illegal in some states, and the federal government is considering imposing a total ban. Any aquarist thinking about acquiring a piranha should check the fish and game laws and consider the dangers involved. Escaped piranhas may survive and reproduce in local waterways, posing a serious threat to the native ichthyofauna.

Group of piranhas (above), and individual specimen

Silver Dollar *(Mylossoma duriventris)*

Family Characidae

The common name silver dollar encompasses a relatively large group of fishes in the family Characidae. All are South American, most from the Amazon basin.

As the name indicates, these fish have round, bright silver bodies. They have some color-changing ability, and during periods of stress and fright, and in courtship, a random scattering of brown or blackish spots may appear on the back, sometimes accompanied by orange-red to blackish spots on the shoulder. All members of the genus *Mylossoma* are schooling fishes, and in the wild it is not unusual to observe groups of more than two thousand individuals. Most silver dollars from the Amazon prefer a temperature range around 75° F (24° C). They swim in open waters and should be given adequate room in the aquarium.

Silver dollars are primarily herbivorous as adults; they accept most prepared foods and relish certain aquarium plants. They will spawn in captivity; the eggs are broadcast much like those of other characins, and they incubate for approximately four days. The young can be fed baby brine shrimp or infusoria until they switch to prepared or plant foods when thirty to forty-five days old.

Hatchet Fish *(Gasteropelecus sp.)*
Family Gasteropelecidae

Several members of this family are popular with aquarists, and all share an unusual ability: they can fly. Other fishes, such as the marine flying fishes and the butterfly fish *Pantodon*, are called fliers but actually only leap. The hatchet fish, through a rapid beating motion of the pectoral fins, is able literally to fly out of the water and glide for three to six meters—a remarkable distance when one considers that the length of the fish is less than two inches (5 cm).

Hatchet fish have deep, compressed bodies and are generally silver-gray with a distinctive narrow dark stripe that runs from the gills to the tail along the lateral line. They have a nearly straight back, and the ventral profile, beginning at the lower jaw and running to the tail, forms a semicircular arch. This enlarged breast region is the site of the powerful muscles that enable the rapid action of the pectoral fins.

These peaceful fish are native to the Amazon and the Guianas. In captivity they prefer soft and slightly acidic water, and will eat most live food, including insect larvae and brine shrimp. They live in the upper portion of the aquarium and coexist well with other fishes.

63

◀ Silver dollar ▲ Hatchet fish

Spraying Characin *(Copella arnoldi)*

Family Lebiasinidae

This unusual but very popular aquarium fish prefers to spawn out of the water. During the mating season a pair of spraying characins will locate a suitable site and literally leap out of the water to spawn from fifty to two hundred sticky eggs. After fertilization, the male tends the eggs and keeps them wet by splashing water with deft and accurate movements of his long tail fin. He continues this activity for two or three days, until the tiny young hatch and fall into the water. In the wild, the undersides of leaves, branches, and roots are favorite spawning sites. In the aquarium, if these objects are absent, the fish will attach the adhesive eggs to the underside of the cover glass.

Spraying characins reach a length of approximately three and a quarter inches (8.25 cm) and have elongate, nearly cylindrical bodies. Their color ranges from dark brown to yellow on the back and yellow-green on the abdomen; the edges of the scales are dark and give the appearance of a netlike covering over the fish. The dorsal fin is long and yellow with a black spot and red tip; the caudal fin, yellow with red edges, has a long upper lobe. The sexes are distinguished by the male's brighter color and longer, more pointed fins.

Spraying characin

Pencil Fish *(Nannobrycon eques)*

Family Lebiasinidae

These small, pencil-shaped fish live in the slow-moving and weedy waters of the middle Amazon and Rio Negro in South America. Surface dwellers, they feed primarily on insects. In the aquarium they will accept almost all live food and most floating prepared diets. Because they are surface feeders, they usually swim slowly with their head up at a 45-degree angle, so that they always look as if they are watching for something to fall into the water. To maintain the head-up position, the caudal fin has an enlarged lower lobe.

Pencil fish are pale gray to silver and have a broad wine-red band that runs from the mouth, over the eyes, and along the body to the lower lobe of the caudal fin. The lower lobe of the fin ends with a black tip; the upper lobe is transparent. At night the horizontal band disappears and is replaced by vertical bars, undoubtedly a form of protective coloration to camouflage the fish while it sleeps.

Pencil fish do well in captivity and have been spawned successfully in aquariums. They lay their eggs a few at a time on fine-leafed plants or the underside of broad-leafed plants until 100 to 150 eggs have been laid over a period of several hours. The young hatch after three days.

Pencil fish

65

Headstander *(Chilodus punctatus)*

Family Curimatidae

This species, widely distributed in northern South America, reaches a length of three inches (7.6 cm) and has the peculiar habit of swimming head-down. At rest, it will position itself at a nearly 45-degree angle. It has a small, upward-pointing mouth, and a thickened upper lip. Its basic color is stone-gray or brown with silver sides; each scale is edged in black, creating a netlike pattern. A black longitudinal band extends from the tip of the mouth over the eye to the middle of the caudal fin.

The headstander has been a popular aquarium fish for many years. It does well in temperatures from 64° to 79° F (18°–26° C) and feeds on small aquatic animals and plants. It has not **66** been bred in captivity.

Headstander

Black-banded Leporinus *(Leporinus fasciatus)*

Family Anostomidae

This species is widely distributed in South America east of the Andes. It is found in nearly every river system from the Guianas and the Orinoco in the north to the Plata in the south.

The black-banded leporinus has a long torpedo-shaped body that may reach twelve inches (30.5 cm) in length, a conical head, and a small mouth. The mouth has the appearance of a harelip, hence the name *Leporinus*, which means "harelike." The color of the body ranges from bright yellow to a dull greenish, with ten black vertical bars. All members of the genus exhibit headstanding behavior, although it is less pronounced than in other genera of the family. They are mainly herbivorous, and in captivity will accept most prepared diets.

Black-banded leporinus

Distichodus *(Distichodus lususso)*

Family Citharinidae

This attractive African characin is an inhabitant of the Congo River and is generally found near the bottom. Several members of this family have become popular aquarium fishes; they will grow to a size of twenty inches (50.8 cm), but their growth rate is slow and it takes several years for them to reach full adult size. The body is typically robust and compressed, with a hunchbacked appearance; the caudal fin is rounded. The basic color ranges from orangeish to nearly red, with six to eight dark transverse bars.

Distochodus are primarily herbivorous and have teeth that are adapted to chew large leaves. Captive specimens will eat plants in the aquarium and will accept a variety of live food and occasionally dry food as well. They prefer a temperature range of 72°–79° F (22°–26° C), and have not been bred in captivity.

In addition to the family Distichodontidae there are two other families of African characins: the Citharinidae, which resemble the South American *Nannobrycon* fishes; and the Ichthyoboridae, small to medium-sized predatory fishes.

Distichodus ▲ Electric eels ▶

Gymnotoidei: Electric Fishes

Electric Eel *(Electrophorus electricus)*
Family Electrophoridae
This cylindrical eel of Central and South America reaches a length of nearly six feet (2 m). It is olive-brown in color, with the underside of the head and jaws orange or red-orange.

Because of their large size and powerful electric discharge, these fish are not popular with home aquarists. If they are kept in an aquarium the tank should be dimly lit and large, as young eels tend to be somewhat belligerent. Electric eels should never be artificially stimulated to discharge current—continual irritation of this kind will cause them to die.

Cyprinoidei: Minnows, Barbs, and Carps

This suborder of Cypriniformes is characterized by the presence of one to three rows of gill teeth on the lower pharyngeal, or throat bones, and the absence of teeth on the jaws and in the mouth. The mouth is protrusile (i.e., it can be extended forward), and the jaws frequently have barbels. Although their fins are generally well developed, Cyprinoidei do not have an adipose (fatty rayless) fin.

The six families of this suborder occur in Africa, North America, Eurasia, and the Indo-Malaysian region. The family Cyprinidae, which includes the minnows, barbs, and carps, gives its name to the suborder and includes more species of fishes than any other family.

Fishes of the genera *Danio* and *Brachydanio* are native to India, Burma, and Southeast Asia. These schooling fishes inhabit both still and flowing waters and are commonly found in rice paddies. All have slim, elongate, compressed bodies. The terminal mouth may face forward or slightly upward. Anal and dorsal fins are always opposite. Many attractive species of these two genera are popular aquarium fishes. In captivity these omnivorous fishes readily accept prepared foods and prefer water temperatures between 68° and 72° F (20°–22° C). During courtship and egg laying they require dense clumps of algae and produce many large eggs, which they shed one at a time in the algae clump. The zebra danio, however, will spawn in an open tank on gravel if no plants are present.

Zebra Danio *(Brachydanio rerio)*
Family Cyprinidae

Introduced in 1905, this native of Burma and India has become a favorite aquarium species. It has a blue body with four golden yellow stripes that extend from the gills to the tail tip. The white-edged anal fin has a similar color and pattern, with three yellow stripes. The opercles, or gill covers, are blue with irregular golden spots, and there are two sets of barbels on the upper jaw. The species breeds well in captivity. The main sexual difference is the female's rounder, wider abdomen.

Zebra danio ▲ Giant danio ▼

Giant Danio *(Danio aequipinnatus)*

Family Cyprinidae

The giant danio, a native of India and Ceylon, is the largest member of its genus. Although wild specimens are usually less than five inches long, some in captivity have grown to eight inches (20.3 cm). The background color is gray-brown to olive-brown and the upper back is blue or blue-green; the abdomen is pink and the head is silvery. It is distinguished from other danios by size and by the three or four blue stripes separated by gold bands which line its flanks. The male is slimmer and brighter in color than the female.

Although the species is peaceful and does well in community tanks, it is well known for its rapid swimming, which can cause the aquarist consternation whenever he or she attempts to catch specimens from the aquarium.

Red Rasbora *(Rasbora heteromorpha)*

Family Cyprinidae

The still and flowing acidic waters typical of the low-lying plains in Southeast Asia and Sumatra are the native habitat of the red rasbora and many other fishes suitable for aquariums. Living compatibly together are such genera as *Barbus, Botia, Hemiramphus, Betta, Trichogaster, Anabas,* and *Brachydanio.*

Although the majority of the rasboras are slim-bodied, the red rasbora's body is relatively short and deep. It is a schooling species, best maintained with its own kind or other closely allied species. The body is silver-gray with a dull red to violet sheen; the abdomen is paler. The posterior portion of the body is marked with a wedge-shaped, blue-black pattern that becomes golden along its anterior edge. The large unpaired fins

Red rasbora ▲ White cloud ▼

are red at the base, shading to yellow along the edges. Females are characterized by a slightly deeper body, a small bulge near the anus, and a fuller abdomen. Many of the young males of this species are bisexual.

Although vegetation is generally scarce in its native habitat, the red rasbora utilizes the shade and protection offered by hanging or floating plants. Courtship consists of the male swimming above the female, who eventually rubs her distended oviduct against broad-leafed plants. In the aquarium she will do this where plant growth is thickest. With the male entwined around her body, she deposits the adhesive eggs on the underside of a leaf. The male fertilizes the eggs as soon as they are laid. The mating period, which always begins in the morning, is broken into several sessions, and as many as three hundred eggs may be deposited by the time it is over. Hatching occurs after forty-eight hours. There is no parental care, and because parents are known to eat eggs and young, most aquarists remove the adults from the tank after fertilization.

White Cloud (Tanichthys albonubes)
Family Cyprinidae

This species, discovered in 1932 in Canton, China, received its common name from the White Cloud Mountains and Tanichthys ("Tan's fish") from the Chinese explorer Tan.

White clouds reach a length of about one and a half inches (3.8 cm); the elongate and moderately compressed body is covered with cycloid (round and smooth) scales. The forward-positioned mouth is located at the tip of the snout and set at an oblique angle. The background color is brownish and the dorsal and anal fins are yellow at the base, shading to red toward the margin. The belly is white, with a brilliant green to golden band extending from the snout to the tail. When the fish is young this band has a bluish green iridescence.

White clouds have become popular and do well in aquariums with temperatures ranging from 50° to about 79° F (10°–26° C), although in their native habitat they can survive in temperatures just above freezing.

Tiger Barb *(Barbus tetrazona)*
Family Cyprinidae

More than half of all cyprinids are barbs, although variation within this group is not as great as it is among danios. Most barbs are bottom-dwellers with elongate, compressed bodies. The mouth, located ventrally, is nearly terminal and there are one or two pairs of barbels on the jaws. The dorsal fin is located in the mid-body or slightly forward, and the anal fin is short. The lateral line is generally straight, ending below the middle of the caudal fin.

Barbs inhabit all types of fresh water, from fast-flowing streams to stagnant ponds. All are egg-layers and most are peaceful fish that do well in large aquariums. In their native habitat, barbs prefer seclusion amid dense aquatic vegetation, so they should be kept in aquariums with dark bottoms,

Tiger barb ▲ Tin foil barb ▼

adequate hiding space, and a quiet population. Because they are not aggressive, they should not be placed in a tank with species that do not have a similar nature.

Tiger barbs, native to Southeast Asia, receive their name from the four black or black-green vertical bars that give a tigerlike appearance. The background color is bright pink to yellowish, with a metallic luster. The back is a darker golden brown, and the abdomen is whitish. The dorsal, anal, and pelvic fins are red, as is the snout.

It is difficult to determine a tiger barb's sex, except at spawning time, when the females have a rounder appearance. If the species is isolated, it can be bred successfully in captivity. (To keep disturbances to a minimum, many aquarists take the other fishes out of the tank rather than move the tiger barb.) During spawning the water temperature should be near 79° F (26° C). Over a period of several hours, the female will lay about five hundred eggs, which hatch in twenty-four hours.

Tin Foil or Schwanenfeld Barb (Barbus schwanenfeldi)
Family Cyprinidae

This large fish, a native of Borneo, Malacca, and Thailand, is often seen in public aquariums. The tin foil's stocky, compressed body appears hunchbacked in older specimens. It has two pairs of barbels. Its uniformly silver body has the appearance of polished aluminum, its color sometimes changing to yellow or gold with the lighting. The red dorsal fin has a black spot on the tip, and the red caudal fin is edged with black on the upper and lower lobes. Unlike many other species, tin foil barbs grow more intense in color as they age.

The tin foil barb grows quite rapidly, and many aquarists are surprised to find that after a few months the streamlined fish they brough home is too large for their aquarium. It is not an aggressive fish, but it can be destructive. Though it will accept "meaty" foods, it is primarily a vegetarian, and without adequate vegetable material it will eat aquarium plants.

Tin foil barbs should be given a large tank with soft acidic water and temperatures between 74° and 78° F (24°–25.5° C). **75**

Red-tailed Shark *(Labeo bicolor)*

Family Cyprinidae

The red-tailed shark is not really a shark; its common name comes from its sharklike appearance. Its soft velvety black color and bright red caudal fin and pectorals make this species a favorite for aquariums. The body is elongate and the ventral profile is nearly straight. Its flaglike dorsal fin and anal and ventral fins are black.

A native of streams in Thailand, it prefers aquariums with some current and a dark environment. Its favorite resting place will be near the filter outlet, facing the incoming water. It eats all kinds of live food and grazes on algae. This species is particularly aggressive with others of its own kind. Unless the aquarium is large enough so that the fish can avoid one another and establish individual territories, it is recommended that only a single specimen be kept. Red-tailed sharks are, however, peaceful with other species and are good community fish.

In the wild these fish inhabit slightly alkaline water with **76** temperatures of 75°–78° F (24°–25.5° C).

Red-tailed shark ▲ Veiltail goldfish ▶

Goldfish *(Carassius auratus)*
Family Cyprinidae

Ever since the introduction of carp into the waterways of Europe (by the Romans) and North America (in the late 1700s), there has been some confusion regarding the difference between carp and goldfish. Both carp and goldfish have been released from captivity and have established "feral," or wild, populations. Under these conditions many casual observers viewing gold-colored fishes misidentify the species involved and attach the most familiar common name, goldfish. Similar mistakes are made by novice birdwatchers who identify all small, dull-colored birds as sparrows. The carp is a member of the genus *Cyprinus*, which is represented by a single species, *Cyprinus carpio*. Goldfish are a distinct and separate species; they belong to the genus *Carassius*, which contains two species. Carp can be distinguished from goldfish by their relatively deep, gray-black or brown bodies, yellow abdomen, and golden or rust-colored sides. Goldfish do not have barbs.

The goldfish, probably native to eastern Asia, is an adaptable and widespread fish. It differs from the second member of

the genus, the crucian carp *(Carassius carassius)*, in several anatomical details such as the scales and gill rakers.

Goldfish have been bred as ornamental fish in China and Japan for more than a thousand years; this we know from a report written in 1136 by a member of the Chinese emperor's court. This breeding has created a striking variety of forms. Some of the popular breeds are the oranda, a colorful fish with a double-tufted tail; the pompom comet, a goldfish whose tail is three times the length of its body; the fringetail, whose tail has the gossamer appearance of fog; the lion head, a Japanese fish with warty growths over the head that create a manelike appearance; and the telescope-eyes.

Generally docile, goldfish become unusually agitated during spawning. Males aggressively rush at females, at times even injuring them. After a frantic chase the female sinks to the bottom, whereupon the male lifts her by pushing with his snout. The female then lays from five hundred to a thousand eggs. Neither parent cares for the young; indeed, if both parents are not removed from the tank they will probably eat the fresh spawn.

In a suitable aquarium goldfish can be expected to live twenty-five to thirty years—the record age is forty. In the wild, they may grow to a length of thirty inches, but in captivity they **78** usually reach no more then ten inches (25.4 cm).

Telescope-eye goldfish

Chinese Algae Eater *(Gyrinocheilus aymonieri)*
Family Gyrinocheilidae

Although closely related to the Cyprinidae, this species belongs to a small family found only in Southeast Asia. The Chinese algae eater is the only gyrinocheilid to have found its way to the aquarium world. This species' most unusual characteristic is its manner of breathing. It does not inhale water through the mouth and pass it over the gills as most other teleosts do; instead, it takes in water through a specialized dorsal gill opening and passes it over the gills then out a lower slit, much as the rays do. This unusual adaptation permits the fish, which lives in rapidly flowing waters, to eat and respire while holding on to algae-covered rocks with its mouth.

Although algae eaters can attain a length of ten inches, in captivity they will not grow much larger than six inches (15 cm) once they have reached sexual maturity.

Clown Loach *(Botia macracantha)*
Family Cobitidae

The loaches are small to medium-sized bottom-dwelling fishes found throughout Eurasia. Their bodies can be short and compact or elongate and cylindrical; all have small heads and tiny eyes covered by a transparent layer of skin. Their ventral mouths are generally surrounded by heavy lips. All loaches have at least three pairs of barbels, the auxiliary pairs being **79**

Chinese algae eaters

well-developed chin flaps that protrude from the mouth. Barbels function as additional tasting organs, and the fishes are constantly testing and tasting in their search for food. The short pectorals are located slightly posterior to the origin of the dorsal fin, which is also short. The body is usually covered with tiny cycloid scales.

Loaches have a good sense of hearing. Some cobitids, such as the weather fish *(Misgurnus fossilis)*, are said to be sensitive to changes in barometric pressure.

The colorful clown loach of the Indo-Australian archipelago has an orange background color accentuated by three blue-black bars. The first bar runs across the eye and the second and third white-edged bars are near the tail. The fins are almost red. The mouth has four pairs of barbels.

Clown loaches, which grow to a length of twelve inches (30.5 cm), do not breed well in captivity. Nevertheless, they are ideal fish for the aquarium because they aid in keeping it clean by eating unwanted algae and surplus food. In captivity their behavior often depends on the number of fishes in the tank. Alone the fish can be quiet and secretive, but when other members are introduced their activity is greatly heightened.

In the wild, this unusual loach sometimes leaves the bottom and hangs on leaves, often in peculiar positions. Its well-developed air bladder allows excellent hydrostatic control, and the fish appears comfortable whether right-side-up or
80 upside-down.

Clown loach

Coolie Loach *(Acanthophthalmus kuhlii)*
Family Cobitidae

This three-inch-long (7.6-cm) eellike fish from India, China, and Malaysia lives in ponds, streams, and canals with muddy or peat bottoms, where it searches for food by rooting around with its mouth and three pairs of barbels. Its entire body, except for the head, is covered with small scales, and it has colorless, nearly transparent, fins. The background color varies from red to orange and is marked by several brown-black vertical bars beginning at the snout and ending at the caudal fin.

Because of their wide geographic distribution, several varieties of *Acanthophthalmus kuhlii* have been identified, but textbooks often disagree as to where the divisions should be drawn. The coolie loach was originally named for a man named Kuhl, who discovered the species. However, the spelling was changed from "kuhli" to "coolie," because so many people, hearing the name and knowing that the fish came from the Orient, automatically assumed it was named for the Indian and Chinese laborers known as coolies.

Coolie loach

Siluriformes: Catfishes

Many people would describe a catfish as a large-headed, whiskered, bottom-dwelling creature inhabiting muddy fresh waters. Although this general description might apply to some types of catfishes, there is enormous variety within this order. There are more than two thousand species in thirty-two families throughout the world, with twelve hundred of these species found in South America. Although the majority are bottom-dwellers, many species are active inhabitants of open water and form schools. Several species inhabit the sea and return to fresh or brackish water to spawn, and a few are strictly marine. They range in size from the doradid, or pygmy, catfishes, which are only a few inches long, to the giant Indian catfish, which grows to a length of ten feet (3 m). One African species, *Malapterurus malapterurus*, is capable of generating a powerful electric charge, and is considered dangerous. Many species have poisonous spines—the first rays of their dorsal and pectoral fins are associated with poison glands.

Catfishes generally do have catlike whiskers around the mouth, which is degenerated and has a weak upper jaw. They do not have true scales, and their body is either naked or covered with a bony armor plate.

Reproduction among catfishes differs in mode, ranging from egg scattering to elaborate nest building to mouth breeding.

There are hundreds of smaller species suitable for the aquarium because of their unique shapes, intriguing behavior, and spectacular coloration.

Striped Dwarf Catfish *(Mystus micracanthus)*
Family Bagridae

The striped dwarf catfish, native to northern India, is naked and lacks the bony armor of some of the other catfishes. It reaches four inches (10 cm) in length. The striped dwarf catfish has four pairs of barbels—the pair located on the upper jaw are much longer than the other pairs, which when bent back will barely reach the pectoral fins. Its mouth is not protrusile and

has toothed jaws.

This fish is matte black or brown in color, with drab bluish white longitudinal bands. It prefers concealment in a well-planted aquarium, with temperatures between 74° and 80° F (24°–27° C). Like most catfishes it is active at dusk and during the evening hours. A good species for the community aquarium, it will accept most food as well as scavenge leftovers. Its breeding habits are not known.

Glass Catfish *(Kryptopterus macrocephalus)*
Family Siluridae

The glass catfish is probably the aquarist's favorite member of this Eurasian family, which includes the European and Asian welses. It does not have the typical catfish appearance or habits. The glass catfish, known as the glass wels in Europe, got its common name from its transparent body. It is easy to discern the internal vertebral bones and ribs, but the head and abdominal cavity are not transparent. Like other transparent fishes, glass catfish become living X-rays when exhibited in aquariums utilizing polarizing filters and light from the rear.

This species, primarily distributed through Indonesia, is distinguished by the single pair of long, forward-projecting barbels. The dorsal fin consists of a single ray, the long anal fin **83**

Striped dwarf catfish

contains seventy rays, and the caudal fin is forked. The species may reach a length of eight inches (20.3 cm).

A schooling fish, the glass catfish prefers open water and does best in aquariums that are not densely planted. In the wild, large schools of glass catfish congregate beneath floating plants and appear to prefer shade to bright light. Whenever a current is present (in the aquarium, there is a "current" next to the filter outlet), the school will swim in unison against the flow. The barbels are in constant motion tasting and testing the environment. Tactile as well as tasting organs, they are also used to maintain position.

Glass catfish are omnivorous and will accept most foods. Large specimens have been known to become rapacious, preying on smaller tankmates.

Walking Catfish *(Clarias batrachus)*
Family Clariidae

The albino phase of this species is a popular aquarium fish despite its predatory habits. Albinos, rare in the animal kingdom, often do not survive except in captivity, but this catfish is one of the few animals in the world that also exists in the wild as an albino. Its normal color is mud brown.

This species has long dorsal and anal fins and an elongate eellike body. The head is broad and flat and has a small, broad, almost terminal mouth with teeth on the jaws and palate bones. The four pairs of barbels are all the same length.

Like many clariids, the walking catfish has small gills and an auxiliary breathing apparatus called a labyrinth, a highly vascular chamber well supplied with blood and located in the

84

Glass catfish

upper rear portion of the gill cavity. The fish ingests air and holds it in the labyrinth while it extracts the oxygen. Because of this special adaptation, walking catfish can inhabit stagnant ponds and even venture overland in search of better environments if their own pool dries or becomes overcrowded. Air breathing also allows survival in less-than-perfect aquariums.

Opportunistic feeders, walking catfish will consume almost any kind of animal flesh, and their rapaciousness has made them the subject of some controversy. Since their recent release in Florida, where they have successfully reproduced, they have been observed "walking" overland from one body of water to another. Their ability to do this has permitted wide distribution over large areas, and their predatory behavior and voracious appetite may have caused irreversible changes in the native ichthyofauna. Importation of this species has been restricted or banned in some states, so consult with local fish and game authorities before obtaining specimens.

Walking catfish ▲ Albino walking catfish ▼

African Upside-down Catfish *(Synodontis nigriventris)*

Family Mochokidae

Anatomically, this native of the Congo River in Africa, as well as other mochokids, can be distinguished from other catfishes by the comblike appearance of the pair of lower-lip barbels. The longest pair of unbranched barbels is on the upper lip. The mouth is inferior and is equipped with rasplike teeth. This species grows no larger than 2¾ inches (7 cm) and does well in temperatures between 68° and 82° F (20°–28° C).

This fish has the interesting habit of constantly swimming on its back. Comfortable in any position, it will rest on one perch normally, then swim to another in an inverted position. Related to this peculiar behavior is its reversed coloration: the shading of its belly is dark, whereas in fishes that swim right-side-up it is usually light. Even feeding and breeding are carried on in this upside-down position.

These hardy fish have a special preference for grazing and spawning on the undersides of leaves of water plants. In captivity, they prefer to spawn in small cavities or caves, where they deposit their adhesive eggs upside-down on the roof. They are scavengers and eat almost anything in the tank, including the algae growing on the glass.

Talking Catfish *(Acanthodoras cataphractus)*

Family Doradidae

This partially armored species from South America has a double row of bony plates along the sides of the body. It has a tadpolelike shape, and reaches six inches (15.2 cm) in length. Typically its coloration is brown to blue-black covered by an irregular pattern of dark spots or lines. The first ray of the dorsal and pectoral fins is a long thornlike spine.

At the bases of the spines in the pectoral fins the bones touch; movement of the fins scrapes the bones together and creates peculiar cricketlike noises, which are amplified by the air bladder. If the fish is removed from the water, it ''talks,'' making noises to indicate its distress.

As with other members of its family, little is known about this fish's breeding habits, though it reportedly has spawned in captivity. Parental care is analogous to that of the species *Amblydoras hancocki*, which builds a bubble nest reinforced with plants.

Small fish, the doradids rarely exceed four inches (10 cm) in length. They prefer a tank temperature of about 75° F (24° C). They are omnivorous, and will clean up scraps and other edible debris in the tank, including dead tankmates.

87

◄ African upside-down catfish ▲ Talking catfish

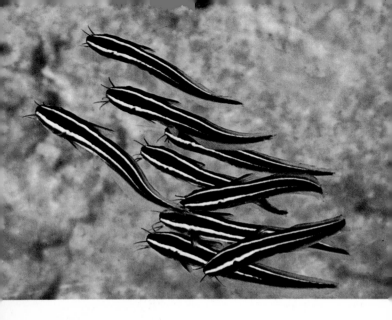

Sea Catfish *(Plotosus anguillaris)*

Family Plotosidae

This is one of the few species of marine catfishes, although some plotosids penetrate into fresh or brackish water. Many catfishes enter the sea but few are able to live in it for their entire life and eventually return to fresh waters.

These catfish have an elongate, torpedo-shaped body, and may reach a length of thirty inches (76.2 cm). Their body is brown with several yellow or whitish stripes. The dorsal fin originates near the head and extends to the caudal fin; the anal fin is nearly as long, joining the dorsal to form a pointed tail. The well-developed dorsal and pectoral spines are associated with a gland which, if pressed, releases a poison that is injected into a victim's skin.

In captivity, the colorful three-inch (7.6-cm) juveniles (adults are generally too large for home tanks) prefer temperatures above 74° F (23° C) and open spaces. In the wild, sea catfish sometimes form large schools made up of thousands of individuals. They will maintain their schooling habits in the aquarium if more than four specimens are present. The school **88** will constantly prowl the bottom searching for leftover food.

Sea catfish

Leopard Corydoras *(Corydoras paleatus)*

Family Callichthyidae

To the aquarium hobbyist, *Corydoras* is the best-known genus of catfishes. The peaceful leopard corydoras of the Rio de la Plata is a member of this very large group found throughout South America.

The upper part of this species' cone-shaped body has two rows of bony armor, which provides protection from predators. The belly is bare. The species reaches a length of three inches (7.6 cm) and has short barbels that project downward from the inferior mouth. The dorsal and pectoral fins have hardened rays, and the spine is used as a defensive mechanism. The caudal fin is forked and the upper lobe is larger than the lower.

The overall color of the species is gray-green to olive, and the back is darker, sometimes appearing blue-black. The back and flanks are covered with dark bluish stripes.

Like many other catfishes this species has an auxiliary respiratory mechanism. It ingests and swallows air and extracts oxygen from it in the lower intestine. During times of stress or high temperatures, corydoras will shoot to the water's surface to gulp air.

Most *corydoras*, including the leopard, are omnivorous and always seem to be searching the bottom for food.

Leopard corydoras

Plecostomus *(Hypostomus plecostomus)*

Family Loricariidae

All members of this South American catfish family live in clear, fresh running water and feed on live vegetation. Loricariids take their name from the Spanish word *lorica*, meaning "armor," because of the bony plates that cover their body. The bony plates that cover this species in overlapping rows provide total protection from predators. The head is shielded by additional bones and the fins protrude between layers of armor. Even during active swimming no bare spots show.

Plecostomus may attain a size of ten inches (25.4 cm) in their native rivers but rarely exceed five or six inches (13–15 cm) in captivity. They are vegetarians and their activities are not only interesting but beneficial to the aquarium. One or two specimens will completely control unwanted algae growth. They should be provided with small rocks, which they will use as resting perches, clinging to them with their suckerlike mouths.

Although this fish is a poor swimmer, jumping from spot to spot along the bottom, it is well adapted to fast-moving water.

90 The specialized sucking mouth and hooked, rasplike teeth are used to hold on to the bottom and to scrape algae from the substrate. Water for respiration is not taken in through the mouth but through the gill opening. This allows the plecostomus to feed or hold on to the bottom and breathe simultaneously. Very little is known about reproduction other than that the male cares for the eggs.

Lophiiformes: Anglerfishes

Sargassum Fish *(Histrio histrio)*
Family Atennariidae

Some of the most unusual marine and deep-sea species belong to this order. They can be distinguished by the presence of a long antennalike ray that attracts prey. The antenna may have a special lure that wiggles or is luminescent.

The sargassum fish is well known in the tropical Atlantic, where it lives in the sargassum weed, the floating alga that gave its name to the Sargasso Sea. Wherever this alga is

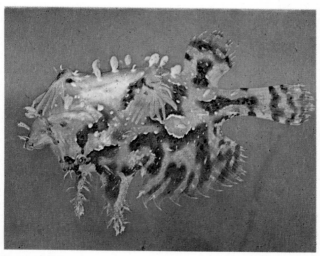

Sargassum fish

present, the fish is there as well; even when clumps of weed drift to shore several fish might be attached. Sargassum fish are well camouflaged by their brown coloration and by numerous skin folds and flaps that create a grotesque appearance, making them nearly identical to the weed.

Although the first ray of the movable dorsal fin is used as a natural bait lure, sargassum fish normally obtain their prey by waiting for small fish to swim by. They eat fishes of their own size, and for that reason young sargassum fish should not be kept together.

The movable pectoral fins are used for a crawling type of locomotion, making these fish poor swimmers. Reproduction of the species is a mystery; a few captive females have laid eggs, but no young have been reared.

Although the sargassum weed will not survive in aquariums for long, these fish do well in captivity. Their carnivorous habits preclude keeping any other fishes of the same size or smaller. Depending on their size, most specimens require live food such as goldfish or guppies.

Atheriniformes: Flying Fishes, Tooth Carps, and Silver Sides

The Atheriniformes comprise a heterogeneous group of fishes, ranging from flying fishes to guppies. Their apparent diversity, however, is only skin deep. They share important anatomical similarities in tooth and jaw structure, and in the bone structure in the head. The group is of marine origin but today contains freshwater forms as well.

Flying fishes are an entirely marine group that received their name because of their habit of sailing over the surface of the sea. No representative aquarium species exists from this group or from the silver sides.

Related to the flying fishes are the half-beaks, fishes with elongate lower jaws. Members of the genus *Hemiramphus* have been successfully maintained by marine aquarists, and *Dermogenys*, an Asian marine form that has been acclimated
to fresh water, is often seen in European aquariums.

Cyprinodontoidei: Tooth Carps

In external appearance, the tooth carps resemble the minnows, barbs, and true carps in many ways. Unlike the Cyprinoidei, however, they have teeth on both jaws and none in the throat, and they do not have barbels.

This group is distributed throughout the world except for Australia and the colder zones north and south of the tropics. Not only do the tooth carps have a wide geographical range, but some species exhibit specialized anatomical and behavioral adaptations, such as dual vision or eggs that survive drought. There are few marine forms, and many estuarine forms return to fresh water to spawn.

The tooth carps are classified by their reproduction methods, which vary from egg laying to live bearing. The egg-layers, known as killi fishes, have the same wide distribution as the suborder. They can be found in both fresh and marine environments. Generally killi fishes are cylindrical.

Reproduction by egg laying is accomplished by external fertilization. The eggs generally develop at a slow rate, and incubation takes two to five weeks. Most species lay their eggs on the surface of fine-leafed plants or on the roots of floating plants. There are some bottom-dwellers that build nests.

Live-bearers of this suborder are ovoviviparous, that is, they produce eggs which hatch within the body, so the young are born live but without placental attachment. This subgroup, found in fresh waters of North, Central, and South America, lives in lakes, rivers, small ponds, and even in puddles remaining after floods. Their bodies have a stubby appearance and are entirely scaled, and they exhibit marked sexual dimorphism. The male is distinguished by his vivid colors.

Panchax *(Aplocheilus panchax)*
Family Cyprinodontidae

This inhabitant of the lowland and coastal waters of India and Southeast Asia first appeared in aquariums in the late 1800s. Colorful and easy to maintain, it soon became a favorite. It has a long, thin, cylindrical body, a flat snout, and a projecting **93** lower jaw. There are at least two varieties within this species. Although color may differ from fish to fish, generally the abdomen is bluish, the body green, and the fin edges orange.

During spawning, eggs are laid in small groups among floating plants and hatch in about thirty days. For successful hatching, the temperature in the tank should be maintained between 64° and 77°F (18°–25°C).

The panchax prefers live food such as insect larvae, daphnia, or tubifex worms. It will occasionally accept some frozen or dried foods as well.

Panchax ▲ Blue gularis (male above) ▼

Blue Gularis *(Aphyosemion coeruleum)*
Family Cyprinodontidae

The blue gularis, which reaches a length of four inches (10 cm), is a native of the slow, stagnant waters of the Cameroon and Niger rivers of Africa. Its long, cylindrical body has a brown-red coloration accented by yellows, greens, and blues in a spectacular pattern that varies in intensity with the breeding season. The large fins, also brilliantly patterned, aid in sex identification as the male's are larger than the female's.

The species prefers a roomy aquarium filled with floating plants. During spawning they seek dark hiding places for their violent and aggressive courtship. The female lays about two hundred eggs on the bottom, preferably on a peat layer. In twenty-five to thirty days the young hatch and must be fed on tiny infusoria. The species eats almost anything that is alive, moving, and small enough to swallow.

Argentine Pearl Fish *(Cynolebias nigripinnis)*
Family Cyprinodontidae

This is one of the so-called annual fishes or, as they are sometimes called, killi fishes. These fishes, in order to survive in areas of annual drought, have developed the ability to hatch, grow, reproduce, and die all within a single season. Members of the genus *Cynolebias* are native to South America; a second cyprinodontoid genus of annual fishes, *Notobranchias,* is found in Africa. Both genera have similar habits and appearances.

Argentine pearl fish, only 2¾ inches (7 cm) long, are characterized by a high, laterally compressed body. The mouth is large and pointed upward, and the jaws have teeth. The large dorsal and anal fins are nearly equal in size, the caudal fin is round, and the pelvic or ventral fins are quite small. Sex is distinguished by the male's larger fins (the dorsal and anal fins are nearly twice as large as the female's) and the female's higher and rounder body.

Because these are subtropical fish, they can withstand cool water—as low as 32° F (0° C) in the wild—but in the aquarium **95**

temperatures should not be allowed to drop below 48° F (9° C). They do best when the water temperature is adjusted to simulate seasonal changes, and breeding is more successful when the water is cooled.

During the courtship and breeding season, which lasts several weeks, the female appears to pursue the male. Once a pair has mated, the male dives head-first into the peat bottom, creating numerous holes. The female then lays nearly one hundred eggs, depositing one egg in each hole. The eggs may remain there for as long as three months before they hatch. In the wild, this long incubation period in the damp peat serves as a protection during periods of drought, when receding waters might otherwise leave the eggs exposed to drying.

Swordtails and Platys (*Xiphophorus sp.*)

Family Poecilidae

Swordtails (*Xiphophorus helleri*) are natives of Central America, inhabiting the rivers that drain into the Caribbean. First taken into captivity in the early 1900s, they have become one of the most popular groups of fishes for the home aquarium. Nearly all swordtails, and their close relatives the platys, are easy to maintain and are admirably suited to aquarium life. Most grow to about three inches (7.6 cm), and **96** thrive on vegetation and most prepared diets. They are peace-

Argentine pearl fish

ful fishes (though the males occasionally fight), and they are remarkably prolific in captivity. *Xiphophorus* species are also easily crossbred, so that hybrids and special strains are constantly being developed. Colors span the spectrum from the green platys to bright red swordtails to albino varieties.

The swordtail is one of the prettiest, easiest to keep, and most easily bred fish available. Even beginning aquarists have no difficult breeding this live-bearing species. Large females may give birth to more than 125 young at a time. The "sword" is a secondary sex characteristic present in males only. Actually an extension of the lower lobe of the caudal fin, it is frequently not as large in special aquarium breeds as it is in wild specimens.

Swordtails (female above)

Platys *(X. maculatus)* are often considered to be suitable only for beginners; many advanced hobbyists no longer maintain the species, although the ease with which it is bred and the potential for developing new strains can lead to a hobby in itself. The platy has been widely used by scientists for genetic studies.

Molly *(Mollienisia latipinna)*
Family Poecilidae

The mollys, like the swordtails and platys and the guppies, exist in numerous varieties and are extremely popular with aquarists. Among the group's notable characteristics are the species' ability to crossbreed with one another, creating new varieties with special traits, such as the high-finned sailfins. Not only do separate species hybridize, *Mollienisia* will crossbreed with other genera such as *Poecilia, Gambusia,* and **98** *Poecilistes,* producing striking hybrids. The black molly, a

Sunset platys (female above)

favorite aquarium fish for many years, was the result of such a cross. Continuous breeding of this form, however, resulted in a reversion in later generations to a fish with white or silver spots.

Native to North and Central America, wild specimens can be caught in the southeastern United States. Mollys do best in aquariums with slightly alkaline, slightly salty water. It has been recommended that salt be added to the tank—about one teaspoonful per gallon—but this limits the other species that can live in the same tank.

The natural habitat consists of shallow bays and estuaries; the species moves freely between fresh and salt water. During the day schools of mollys migrate into very shallow, warm water, 74°–86° F (23°–30° C), to feed and breed. They are omnivorous, though vegetable matter makes up the bulk of their diet. In captivity they do well on prepared dry foods.

A large, densely planted tank is required for breeding. A single pair can produce as many as 120 live young. The young are fairly large and grow rapidly, but the large fin of the male does not develop until he reaches sexual maturity. **99**

Molly

Guppy *(Poecilia reticulata)*

Family Poecilidae

The vast majority of aquarium hobbyists begin their first aquariums with guppies. These hardy little fish—females grow to two and a half inches (6.4 cm), males to only one and a half (3.8 cm)—are easy to care for and tolerate varying water conditions and temperatures. They prefer a tank filled with vegetation and eat almost anything, including their own new-born young.

Sexual differentiation is quite apparent in guppies. Besides being smaller than the female, the male is more brightly colored and has a compressed, enlarged tail and a proportionately larger dorsal fin. The guppy's basic body color is silver-gray to green, with the fins ranging from blue-green to blue to yellow to red to various combinations of these, depending on the particular strain or variety.

Guppies breed when very young, even before they have attained full color, and they are quite prolific. The rapidity of reproduction allows even the beginning aquarist to practice selective breeding techniques in order to obtain special strains. Serious hobbyists separate the young from the parents to prevent cannibalism, and then separate the males from the females for selection of color and body and fin size.

Squirrel fishes

Beryciformes: Squirrel Fishes, Pine Cone Fishes, and Deep-sea Berycoids

Squirrel Fish *(Holocentrus sp.)*

Family Holocentridae

Squirrel fishes, found exclusively in salt water, are world-wide tropical fishes belonging to the order Beryciformes. Unlike many members of this order, squirrel fishes prefer shallow water. All seventy members of the family Holocentridae are some shade of red, with color patterns ranging from red with black bars to red with peppermintlike stripes. Coarse ctenoid (rough-edged) scales cover the body, and the dorsal and anal fins and gill covers are armed with strong spines. In some species the spines are associated with a gland that produces a mild poison.

Nearly all squirrel fishes are nocturnal and hide in crevices and under ledges of the coral reef during the day; at night they leave these crevices to feed on swarming crustaceans.

Holocentrus ensifer and *H. ascensionis,* shown here, attain a length of twelve inches (30.5 cm), and juveniles are regularly captured for aquariums. They have not yet been bred in captivity.

101

◄ Guppies (female at right) and young

Gasterosteiformes: Sticklebacks and Sea Horses
Shrimp Fish *(Aeoliscus strigatus)*
Family Centriscidae

This headstanding tropical marine fish inhabits the Indo-Pacific from the Persian Gulf east to Hawaii. The species is easily distinguished by its habits and unusual appearance. It has a very elongated body, severely compressed along the abdominal ridge and covered not with scales but with a bony armor similar to that of the pipe fishes and sea horses. The caudal fin is arched downward and has the appearance of a normal anal fin, and the tail is formed by a long dorsal fin spine rather than by the caudal fin. The mouth is at the end of a long tubular snout. The abdomen has a sharp edge that may be utilized in aggressive behavior. The color is a striking mixture of wine-red on the dorsal side and yellow along the belly. There is a long black longitudinal band running the length of the body, and each of the bony plates has three silver spots.

The shrimp fish maintains the headstanding position whenever it is at rest; only when hunting does it swim horizontally like other fishes. When threatened, a shrimp fish will position itself among the long spines of sea urchins, making it difficult and even painful for a predator to attempt capture. Apparently it also feeds on small crustaceans that live among

Shrimp fish ▲ Sea horses ▶

the urchins' spines and the coral: its long tubelike snout is perfectly adapted for searching the crevices for food.

Shrimp fish are a schooling species and do very well in captivity. They feed on live brine shrimp as well as some of the freeze-dried prepared foods. They do best in very clean water at temperatures between 75° and 80° F (24°–27° C).

Sea Horse *(Hippocampus hudsonius)*
Family Syngnathidae

The world of fishes is filled with strange and bizarre forms, each unique and specialized for a distinct mode of life. Among the more bizarre fishes, none is more popular than the sea horse. Members of this family, which include the pipe fishes, have bodies encased in rings of bony armor, and mouths located at the end of long tubular snouts.

The sea horse's head is perpendicular to its arched body, and it swims in an upright position. Its small pectoral fins are located immediately behind the tiny, tufted gill openings. There are no pelvic or caudal fins; the sea horse swims by utilizing the wavy motions of the pectorals. The prehensile tail, generally curled up, is used to grasp coral or seaweed so that the fish can maintain a steady position while it waits for its prey, generally small crustaceans or juvenile fishes. Most sea horses are brown to greenish in color, though there is one

Pacific form that is bright yellow.

Perhaps the most unusual feature of the sea horses and pipe fishes is the male's abdominal incubation pouch. During the breeding season the female deposits up to two hundred eggs in this pouch, where they are fertilized and incubated by the male for four weeks. As the eggs hatch and the young escape from the pouch, the male appears to go through labor pains and contractions.

The record length of time sea horses have been maintained in captivity is about two years; it is currently believed that this is near their maximum life span.

Scorpaeniformes: Scorpion Fishes

Lion Fish (Pterois volitans)

Family Scorpaenidae

Lion fishes, also known as turkey fishes or zebra fishes, are probably the most popular representative of the order Scorpaeniformes, a large group of small to medium-sized marine fishes. (A few freshwater species exist, but they are not popular aquarium fishes.) Seven or eight species of lion fishes inhabit the coral reefs of the tropical Indo-Pacific. Their pectoral and dorsal fins are large in proportion to the body, which may reach fifteen inches (38 cm) in length, and the rays and spines are separated. The dorsal fin is divided and has thirteen bony spines and ten or eleven rays.

All lion fishes are predators, and their coloration, red-brown with white zebra stripes, provides effective camouflage as they perch in the corals awaiting their prey. They attack by spreading the pectoral fins into a fan which herds the prey into place.

Lion fishes must be handled with care, for, like many other members of their family, they are poisonous. At the base of each long dorsal spine there is a group of poison-producing cells, and when one of the spines punctures an enemy's skin, it bathes the wound with poison, causing extreme pain, tissue damage, shock, and possibly even death. The spines are not **104** used solely for defense; the species is aggressive and may attack an unwary victim. If a lion fish in the aquarium is seen with its head tilted down, tail up, and spines raised, it should be approached with extreme caution—this is the posture the fish assumes when it is about to attack. Fortunately, an attack need not be lethal. The wound can be detoxified by immersing the injured part in hot water. Deep puncture wounds, of course, should receive immediate medical attention.

Lion fishes

Perciformes: Perchlike Fishes

The order Perciformes constitutes the largest group of fishes in the world, with representatives in nearly all of the world's fresh and salt waters. In variety, number of species, and diversity of habit, this may be considered the most successful present-day order of fishes. It is divided into 150 families and 6,000 known species, including the world's largest and smallest fishes.

Percids have two dorsal fins, the first being made up of bony spines and the second of softer rays. There is a distinct difference between these spines and rays: spines are bones of a singular structure, whereas rays are jointed. The pectoral fins are located on the throat or chest and the anal fin is short, generally consisting of three spines located in front of the soft rays. The caudal fin never has more than seventeen complete rays. These fishes may or may not have an air bladder; if it is present, it is never connected to the intestine. All Percids lack intermuscular bones, which makes them popular food fishes.

Cony ▲ Royal gramma ▼

Cony *(Cephalopholis fulva)*
Family Serranidae

Conies are members of the family Serranidae, or basses, which includes the largest fishes in the world, the groupers and black sea basses. Very few serranids are suitable for the aquarium because of their large size and their predatory habits.

The cony, a native of the western Atlantic, is a small sea bass, reaching a maximum length of sixteen inches (41 cm). It can be kept in a large home aquarium, but should not be placed in a tank with smaller fishes as it will probably eat them. Its color ranges from yellowish to orange-brown, with dark-edged blue spots covering the body. Like many other sea basses, conies undergo sex reversal. All individuals are born female and become male after five or six years.

Royal Gramma *or* **Fairy Basslet** *(Gramma loreto)*
Family Grammidae

All members of this family are strikingly colored reef fishes with small, elongate bodies that reach a maximum length of four inches (10 cm). The most common aquarium species in the group, the royal gramma, is from the Caribbean. It can be distinguished by the brilliant purple coloration on the anterior portion of its body and the golden yellow coloration on the posterior. There is also a black spot on the anterior portion of the dorsal fin.

The royal gramma is a solitary species, preferring to live in the holes and caves common in coral reefs. In the aquarium it should be given a variety of secretive hiding places; it can often be seen perching upside-down in the refuge of its choice. Royal grammas are carnivorous, feeding on the macro-zooplankton that abounds in the coral reef. Reluctant to feed in captivity, they are usually acclimated with live food such as small fishes or brine shrimp.

Because of their dietary preferences, royal grammas are not among the easier marine fishes to maintain. Despite its color and attractiveness, this species should not be among the beginning aquarist's first choices.

Flame Fish *(Apogon maculatus)*

Family Apogonidae

The apogonids, or cardinal fishes, are a family of small, color-ful reef fishes inhabiting all the tropical seas of the world. A few species inhabit brackish water and one, *Apogon trifaciatus* of New Guinea, lives in fresh water. Many are cardinal-red in color, hence their name. The body is generally covered with ctenoid scales, and there are two dorsal fins, giving these fishes a distinctive appearance. The eyes and head are large in proportion to the body—the lower jaw projects forward and the mouth has small teeth on the jaws, palate, and tongue.

The flame fish, which ranges from Florida to Brazil, is red with a black spot at the base of the second dorsal fin and black spots near the eye. A nocturnal predator in the wild, it gener-ally seeks shelter during the day. However, it adjusts readily to aquarium life and soon begins coming out to feed and swim about during daylight hours. As predators, flame fish feed on small fish and macro-plankton; in captivity they will eat live brine shrimp, frozen brine shrimp, and other freeze-dried preparations.

Flame fish are mouth brooders. The eggs are fertilized exter-nally and are then carried in the male's mouth for the incuba-tion period. They have not bred in captivity, and details of courtship, egg laying, and brooding time are not known.

Flame fish

Pork Fish *(Anisotremus virginicus)*

Family Pomadasyidae

Pork fish, found in the tropical western Atlantic, belong to the family known as the grunts, all of whose members are marine. Among the noisiest fishes in the sea, the grunts take their name from the characteristic sound they produce by grating teeth located in the throat. The sound is amplified by the air bladder, and the resulting loud noises can be heard clearly through the aquarium walls without special listening devices.

Grunts have the typical body shape of the percid fishes; however, the teeth are small and there are no palate teeth on the roof of the mouth. Like many other members of its family, the pork fish has very different color patterns as a juvenile and as an adult. The young pork fish has a yellowish head and white body with two black horizontal stripes beginning near the gill covers and extending to the caudal peduncle. There is a black spot at the base of the tail, and the fins are yellow. Adults have the same body shape and whitish background color, but the horizontal stripes are blue and yellow rather than black, and are less defined. The fins remain yellow, but two vertical black bars develop. Pork fish reach a size of about twelve inches (30.5 cm); the color change occurs when they are between three and four inches in length. They are common reef fishes, and the young pick parasites from other fishes. **109**

Pork fish

Sweet lips ▲ Spotted sweet lips ▼ Cubbyu ▶

Sweet Lips (*Plectorhynchus orientalis*)

Family Pomadasyidae

This colorful genus of grunts inhabits the tropical Indo-Pacific and until recently was classed in a separate family. They live in large schools in shallow water and, like many other members of the family, have different juvenile and adult color patterns. The juveniles have black and white spots, which are often edged with yellow; the adults have a white body with black stripes and yellow dorsal and ventral fins.

The sweet lips is a prized aquarium specimen because of its attractive colors, ease of care, and diversified diet. It will accept a wide variety of live and frozen foods, such as shrimp, fish, and clams. Like most marine fishes, it has not been bred in captivity, and relatively little is known about its reproductive **110** habits.

Cubbyu *or* **High Hat** *(Equetus acuminatus)*

Family Sciaendae

Like the grunts, the sciaenids, or drums, make noises loud enough to be heard outside the aquarium or by divers swimming in the ocean. The drums produce these sounds not with teeth as the grunts do, but by rapid vibration of muscles attached to the air bladder. The sounds are used for species identification, particularly during the spawning season.

The high hats and their relatives occur only around tropical reefs of the West Indies. The body is triangular and may reach a length of nine inches (23 cm). The dorsal fin is long and membranous and may be as high as one-half the total body length. These proportions change as the fish matures; the fin is shorter in older specimens. The coloration is basically white or yellowish with dark longitudinal bars, the most prominent one beginning on the anterior edge of the dorsal fin.

These nocturnal fish do very well in captivity and have been bred in public aquariums. Sex determination is nearly impossible unless egg laying is observed. Courtship consists of head-to-tail chasing, circular swimming, and body rubbing. The female lays several hundred eggs, which sink into the sand after fertilization by the male and hatch in four to six days. **111**

Yellow Goatfish *(Mulloidichthys martinicus)*

Family Mullidae

The family Mullidae comprises about forty marine species distributed world-wide throughout the tropical and warm temperate regions. Only a few species are found in aquariums.

The yellow goatfish is a bottom-dwelling schooling species, easily distinguished by two long fleshy barbels located on the lower jaw. These movable appendages are well supplied with nerve, taste, and tactile cells. The fish digs through the sand with these barbels to locate prey such as worms, crustaceans, and mollusks. When the fish is swimming rapidly and the barbels are not in use, they lie back in the grooves of the lower jaw. The body is elongate, with a large head, a small mouth, and protrusile jaws. The dorsal fin is divided into two separate fins, the first having weak spines. The caudal fin is forked.

In the aquarium, goatfish swim about the bottom using their barbels to search for food. Upon finding a particle of food, the goatfish extends its jaws and simply sucks the object up. This activity does not disturb the sand and helps to keep the tank clean. Goatfish feed on all types of fish flesh, as well as shrimp and brine shrimp. Tank temperatures should be maintained near 75° F (24° C).

Yellow goatfish ▲ Finger fish ▶

Finger Fish *(Monodactylus argenteus)*
Family Mondactylidae

Monodactylus, the only genus in the family Monodactylidae, consists of five species of schooling fishes of remarkably similar appearance. All are referred to as finger fishes. Their distribution is limited to the tropics, where they are generally found in estuaries associated with mangroves. Finger fishes are among the few fishes seen in both freshwater and marine aquariums; *M. argenteus,* which is found in Australia, Malaysia, Indonesia, and the Indian Ocean west to Africa, is the most common aquarium species.

Almost nothing is known about the reproduction or courtship habits of this species. Sexually immature juveniles, which look just like the adults except that they are smaller, are frequently found in fresh and brackish water. The body is flat and circular and may attain a maximum length of eight inches (20 cm). It has a silver mother-of-pearl background color with two black stripes on the head. The dorsal and anal fins, triangular with broad bases, are black at the anterior edges. The caudal fin is broad, and all median fins are light yellow.

In the wild, finger fishes feed on both plant and animal material. They will accept a wide variety of live and prepared foods in the aquarium.

Archer Fish *(Toxotes jaculator)*

Family Toxotidae

Archer fishes are equally at home in fresh or salt water. As long as the water is warm, between 72° and 79° F (22°–26° C), they can live comfortably and reproduce in either environment. The most common species, *Toxotes jaculator*, occurs in the Red Sea, Indian Ocean, and throughout Indonesia.

T. jaculator grows to a maximum size of about eight inches (20 cm). The entire body is scaled, and the basic color is yellow or gray-green, with the back darker than the abdomen. This color is accentuated by four to six dark bars extending halfway down the body from the top of the back. The back profile is nearly straight.

Archer fishes were given their name because of their unusual manner of hunting for food. With remarkable accuracy, they shoot jets of water out of their mouths, much as an archer shoots arrows, to knock prey from leaves and overhanging branches. The archer fish has large eyes with which to search out the small insects on which it feeds. Once it has its prey in view, it swims into position, placing its snout just above the surface, and adjusts its body until it is in line for a shot. By pressing its large, fleshy tongue against the roof of its mouth, which is grooved, the fish forms a barrel with its mouth. Through rapid muscular contractions the gill covers are compressed and water is forced through the barrel. In captivity, these fishes will demonstrate their "shooting" ability if worms, flies, and other insects are placed above the water level.

Archer fish   Bat fish ▶

Bat Fish *(Platax pinnatus)*

Family Ephippidae

The brilliance of its velvety black body and contrasting red forehead and yellow-edged fins, combined with its graceful swimming movements and elegant shape, have made this species one of the favorites of marine aquarists.

These tropical Indo-Pacific fish are found in quiet waters of coral reefs and mangrove swamps. The juveniles differ from adults in shape and color. Juveniles have much longer dorsal, anal, and pelvic fins and are actually taller from the tip of the dorsal to the bottom of the anal fin than they are long. As the fish matures these proportions change, and the entire body takes on a more rounded appearance. The coloration of juveniles is also more brilliant; adults appear darker.

These fish are graceful swimmers, sometimes surprising

observers with the intricate maneuvers they execute in order to obtain food. They also "play dead" and drift in the current like a leaf. Bat fish are among the few species that can become tame enough to be real "pets"—often they will accept food directly from the aquarist's hand.

All aquarium specimens are captured wild, and nothing is known about their courtship or breeding behavior. Small specimens quickly acclimate to tank life and feed on any type of chopped fish, shrimp, or scallops. They prefer tank temperatures near 79° F (26° C).

Spotted Scat *(Scatophagus argus)*
Family Scatophagidae

This common scat lives in fresh, brackish, and marine environments and can be found in nearly every harbor in the tropical Indo-Pacific region. All scats are black and white or black and silver and have a deep notch between the spiny and soft portions of the dorsal fin. The body is compressed and covered with small ctenoid scales. The head and mouth are small and the teeth are set in bands on the jaws.

As the name *Scatophagus* (in Greek, literally "dung-eater") indicates, scats will eat nearly anything. They are schooling fishes, and if several small specimens are maintained together they will demonstrate schooling behavior in the tank.

Spotted scat

Very little is known about the spotted scat's courtship and breeding behavior. It is believed that the adults leave the harbors and mangrove swamps to breed offshore. The young inhabit fresh water for the first part of their lives, then, when sexually mature, adopt a harbor and estuarine existence. Though they will live in fresh water, their color is brighter in brackish or salt water. In freshwater tanks their diet must contain adequate plant material. If it does not, they will eat the tank decorations. Whether fresh or salt, the water should be close to 75° F (24° C).

Amazon Leaf Fish (Monocirrhus polyacanthus)
Family Nandidae

Members of this interesting freshwater family are found in northern South America, the Congo drainage basin in Africa, and India and Southeast Asia. All nandids are known for their predatory habits—they are capable of eating fishes nearly three-quarters their own size. They can be kept with fishes their own size or larger, but they must always be adequately fed, for they are voracious and consume their own weight in food each day.

The Amazon leaf fish's manner of stalking prey is rather unusual; it does not actively search but waits patiently and motionlessly for the food to come to it. Camouflaged not only by its coloration, which changes to match the greens and browns of the surrounding environment, the leaf fish also has a long chin barbel that resembles a stem. Mimicking a dead leaf, it drifts with the current in a head-down position until an unsuspecting victim ventures near and is sucked in by the large protrusile mouth.

Leaf fishes spawn on large plant leaves and stones which are cleaned by the male before the eggs are laid. The male assumes the task of guarding, fanning, and cleaning the eggs, which hatch in three to four days. In the aquarium the young should be isolated as the cannibalistic parents may eat their own offspring. Within a few days the young will begin eating their siblings, so they too must be separated.

117

Several other members of this family are popular aquarium fishes. The blue perch *(Badis badis)* is probably the most docile and is not as predatory as the leaf fish. Although it eats large quantities of food, its small mouth prevents it from eating fishes near its own size.

Family Chaetodontidae: Butterfly Fishes and Angel Fishes

Very few animals match the brilliant colors and beauty of these tropical marine fishes of the coral reef. Of all the fishes inhabiting the tropics, the butterfly and angel fishes are the most attractive and the most readily available candidates for the marine aquarium.

The family, which includes more than 150 species, is generally divided into two subfamilies: butterfly fishes (Chaetodontinae) and angel fishes (Pomacanthinae). Butterfly fishes are small to medium-sized, rarely exceeding eight inches (20.3 cm) in length. They have high backs, compressed bodies, and numerous flexible comblike teeth set in both jaws. The snout is more or less elongate, and in some species, such as the long-nosed butterfly fish *(Forcipiger flavissimus),* it is extremely long and tapered and is used to obtain food lodged between the crevices and branches of the sharp corals. Angel **118** fishes are generally larger, some species growing to nearly two

Amazon leaf fish

feet (61 cm). In addition, they are distinguished by the presence of a long hard spine, lacking in the butterfly fishes, located on the lower edge of the preopercle, the small bone located in front of the gill opening. The dorsal fin is frequently longer than the butterfly fishes'.

The family is exclusively marine, distributed through all the tropical seas of the world. A few species enter brackish water but return to the sea for reproduction. Almost all members of the family are solitary or live in pairs; only one species, *Chaetodon larvatus,* found in the Red Sea, can be considered a schooling species.

In the aquarium, chaetodontids prefer water temperatures around 75° F (24° C). They are diurnal—active in the daytime, hiding and sleeping at night—and most are peaceful and nonaggressive. Some, however, are territorial, and if there is inadequate space in the tank they will fight with other members of their own species.

Little is known about the courtship and reproduction of the family, since they have not been bred in captivity. Oceanographers have found that after spawning and fertilization, the eggs float to the surface and the young are hatched as larvae. After a few weeks these larvae metamorphose into adult-appearing fish and settle to the bottom.

Four-eye Butterfly Fish (Chaetodon capistratus)

Family Chaetodontidae

This is one of the most common reef inhabitants of the West Indies and Florida. During the warm summer months it may venture as far north as Cape Cod. Its close relative, the golden butterfly fish (*C. auriga),* has a much wider range, including east Africa and the central Pacific, but does not do as well in captivity as the four-eye.

The four-eye's common name refers to the false eyespots located near the tail. An obliterative black eyebar conceals the fish's true eyes, so that predators are deceived into thinking that the tail is the head. While its tail is being attacked, the four-eye has time to dart away out of danger. **119**

Like many other butterfly fishes, this species is often seen in pairs in the ocean, and two or more do well in an aquarium. Peaceful fish, they get along well with tankmates of other species. Even though their range is farther north than any other butterfly fish, they require temperatures above 70° F (21.6° C).

Four-eye butterfly fish have small mouths and feed on live brine shrimp and finely chopped fish or shrimp. They will also accept freeze-dried shrimp and brine shrimp. They appear to be picky feeders; they eat slowly and do best if fed small meals several times a day.

Four-eye butterfly fish ▲ Golden butterfly fish ▼

Long-nosed Butterfly Fish *(Forcipiger flavissimus)*
Family Chaetodontidae

Distributed from eastern Africa and the Red Sea east to Hawaii and the west coast of North America, this butterfly fish has the widest range of any member of the family. Generally associated with coral reefs, long-nosed butterfly fish are also found among rock outcrops. The long nose is adapted to feeding in the crevices of the rocks and coral and picking up small invertebrates.

This species is territorial and quite aggressive with others of its own kind. Occasionally an aquarist can observe a long-nosed butterfly fish using its dorsal spines as offensive weapons. Swimming on its side with its dorsal fin erect, it will stab an opponent with its spines.

Although this species does not have distinct false eyespots, there is a spot on the tail, and the profile of the caudal region looks enough like the head of other butterfly fishes to deceive some potential predators.

The brilliantly attractive long-nose is one of the more popular chaetodontids. It does very well in captivity and gets along well with other species. Since it will grow to six inches (15.2 cm), it requires a relatively large tank. After a few weeks in the aquarium, it will start coming to the surface for food. Its diet should be varied, consisting of such foods as live brine shrimp, freeze-dried brine shrimp, and finely chopped fish and shrimp. The aquarium water should be very clean and maintained at a temperature above 74° F (23° C). **121**

Long-nosed butterfly fish

Heniochus or **Banner Fish** *(Heniochus acuminatus)*

Family Chaetodontidae

This butterfly fish is distinguished by its steep body, high arched back, long filamentous dorsal fin, and striking coloration. Strong white and black vertical bands cross the body, and the soft dorsal and caudal fins are tinged with yellow. Members of the genus live throughout the tropical Indo-Pacific.

One of the more common members of its family seen in marine aquariums, this species is sometimes confused with and even sold as the moorish idol. Whereas the latter is very difficult to keep, however, the banner fish is easy to care for. Like bat fish, banner fish become quite tame and can be somewhat gluttonous. They will accept almost any food offered and do well on a mixed diet of chopped fish, shrimp, and live and frozen brine shrimp.

The banner fish requires clean water and temperatures above 74° F (23° C). Since its long dorsal fin is one of its more striking characteristics, some care must be exercised in selecting appropriate tankmates—notorious fin nippers such as the damsel fishes must be avoided.

Banner fish

Queen Angel Fish (*Holocanthus ciliaris*)

Family Chaetodontidae

The genus *Holocanthus* contains the majority of the angel fishes. The queen angel fish is a native of the tropical western Atlantic and Gulf of Mexico and attains a size of about seventeen inches (43.2 cm). The color pattern of the juveniles differs from that of adults. Juveniles have three light blue bars on the body and two light blue bars on the head, bordering a dark bar that runs through the eye. These bars begin to fade when the fish is three inches (7.6 cm) long, and the pattern is replaced by the splendid and distinctive coloration of the adult.

Normally a shallow-water species, the queen angel fish adapts readily to aquarium conditions. Omnivorous in the wild, it accepts all types of food, including chopped fish and shrimp and live and frozen brine shrimp. It will also graze on algae. Its brushlike teeth are adapted for scraping algae and other encrusted growth off rocks and coral.

Queen angel fish juvenile ▲ and adult ▼

123

Rock Beauty *(Holocanthus tricolor)*

Family Chaetodontidae

Another tropical western Atlantic species, the rock beauty can be found from Georgia and Bermuda through the Caribbean and the West Indies. The bright yellow color of the front portion of the body appears to flow out and over the edges of all the fins. The dorsal and anal fins, and most of the rest of the body, are covered by a large black patch. The eyes have bright blue edges on the upper and lower iris. When they are young, rock beauties are all yellow except for a blue-edged black spot just behind the midpoint on the upper side of the body. It is this black spot that expands to create the adult coloration. The species attains a size of ten to twelve inches (25.4–30.5 cm).

Rock beauties are regularly imported and are generally less expensive than the more exotic angel fishes. Because they are initially very timid, they require an aquarium that has sufficient shelter. After a few days of acclimation they will come out of hiding, but even then they will immediately dart back in at the first sudden movement or loud noise.

A basic diet of fish, shrimp, and brine shrimp should be supplemented with algae or finely chopped spinach. Some aquarists permit algae to grow on the back wall of the tank to provide the necessary vegetation. The water temperature should be maintained above 74° F (23° C).

Rock beauty

Family Cichlidae: Cichlids

Cichlids are distributed throughout the tropical and subtropical regions of Asia, Africa, and North, Central, and South America. The family contains over six hundred species, more than a hundred of which are suitable for aquariums. They are almost exclusively freshwater fishes. The few exceptions are several brackish-water species in the genera *Tilapia* and *Cichlasoma,* and the Indian genus *Etropus,* all of whose members are found in brackish water.

A distinctive characteristic of the cichlids is their single nostril. Members of the family may be long and slim, like the pike cichlids, or have deep and compressed bodies, like the freshwater angel fish and the discus. The head is generally large in comparison with the rest of the body, and the body is covered with ctenoid scales. Many species have large eyes, and some develop fatty or bumpy foreheads as they mature.

The courtship and reproduction patterns of these fishes have been studied by animal behaviorists, such as Konrad Lorenz, who are seeking to learn more about pairing, territoriality, and parent-young recognition. Fertilization is external, and parental care ranges from simple spawning to elaborate mouth brooding of eggs and young. In the case of mouth brooders, after the mature fish pair, a nesting pit is dug by the male or both partners. Once the female has spawned in the nesting pit, the male or female will pick up the eggs and hold them in a special throat pouch for brooding. In some species the eggs are picked up by the female immediately after they are laid, and fertilization occurs in the female's mouth after she puts on an elaborate behavioral display that stimulates the male to spawn. Usually the brooding parent does not feed, but a few species will eat a small amount during the incubation period. After hatching, the young are cared for by the parent and frequently return to the parent's mouth to seek shelter.

Many cichlids are predatory and grow to a large size and so cannot be maintained in community tanks. However, there are, among the six hundred members of the family, many small and docile species whose interesting mode of life has made them favorites with aquarists.

Egyptian Mouth Breeder *(Haplochromis multicolor)*

Family Cichlidae

This native of northern and eastern Africa is abundant throughout the shallow waters of the Nile River drainage from Alexandria to Lake Victoria. It is one of the more popular aquarium cichlids. The body is moderately high and laterally compressed, reaching a size of three and a half inches (9 cm). The mouth is large and directed upward and the fins are all well developed, with the caudal fin large, rounded, and fan-shaped. The basic coloration is yellow-green to yellow-brown, with an overall purple-blue sheen. The back is darker and shades to a lighter silver-yellow on the abdomen. In the males, the anal fin is tipped with red. During the mating season this red spot becomes brighter, and the male's body

becomes more intensely blue. The head and gill covers turn yellow, the throat black, and the scales golden. The female's coloration does not change.

During courtship the male drives the female into a hole or trench nest that he has excavated and cleaned. Both partners engage in a great deal of circling, nudging, and head-to-tail positioning, after which the female lays twenty to one hundred eggs in groups of five to twelve at a time. The male fertilizes the eggs in the nest and the female picks them up for brooding. The female's throat sac is semitransparent, so the eggs are visible throughout the incubation period, which lasts ten to fourteen days. During this time the female does not eat, but after the young are hatched she feeds them by chewing up her own food and spitting it out for them.

This species is the smallest of its genus and the most readily available to the aquarist. Because of its small size, it is a fairly safe species to introduce into a community aquarium. It will do well in acidic, neutral, or even slightly alkaline water at temperatures ranging from 74° to 80° F (23°–27° C). Live and frozen foods such as daphnia, tubifex worms, and brine shrimp are preferred, though dry diets are accepted as well.

Blue Acara (Pelmatochromis subocellatus pulcher)
Family Cichlidae

This three-and-a-half-inch-long (9-cm) acara lives in the Niger River delta region of Africa. There appear to be at least seven or eight varieties of this species which are capable of crossbreeding. The differences in the coloration of these varieties seem to be adaptations to the geographical conditions in the particular areas they inhabit. The basic coloration of the species is purple-red to violet; some varieties possess single eyespots, in some the spots occur in multiples, and in some they are absent entirely.

During the breeding season the male digs a pit or a cave and cleans all surfaces in preparation for egg laying. Some aquarists place upturned flower pots in the tank to be used as nesting sites. The pair engages in false spawning behavior for **127**

◀ Egyptian mouth breeders

nearly two weeks before the eggs are laid. The parents place the adhesive eggs on all surfaces of the nest, including the ceiling if there is one. The female alone fans and cleans the eggs while they incubate, and the male, driven from the nest, remains nearby. Both parents defend the nest and the young after hatching. The parents should be separated from their offspring at about the time the young leave the nest, for parental care ceases at this point, and the adults are likely to eat most of the brood.

This species includes the fish formerly known as *P. pulcher*, *P. taeniatus*, and *P. kribensi*. They are peaceful aquarium fish that require soft, slightly acidic water and temperatures between 76° and 80° F (24°–27° C). Their food requirements can be satisfied with live or prepared diets.

Fire Mouth Cichlid (*Cichlasoma meeki*)

Family Cichlidae

This species is probably the most popular aquarium cichlid in the United States. *Cichlasoma*, the largest cichlid genus, contains sixty to seventy species which are native to the marshes, lakes, and rivers of North, Central, and South America. Nearly all can be kept in aquariums.

The fire mouth is a common inhabitant of the streams and ponds of the Yucatan Peninsula of Mexico. It reaches a length of three inches (7.6 cm), and the body is high and laterally compressed. The forehead is steep, the snout sharp, and the mouth upturned. Fire mouths are blue-gray to violet acrosss the body and back, with scales edged in red or red-brown. The

Blue acara ▲ Fire mouth cichlid ▶

belly, throat, part of the gill covers, and the interior of the mouth are orange-red. Irregular black spots occur on the edge of the opercles, which are bordered with iridescent shades of white, green, or yellow. The dorsal, anal, and caudal fins are blue-gray with white spots. The dark vertical bars across the body disappear with changes in behavior associated with feeding, breeding, and fright. The female's colors are not as vivid as the male's.

During courtship the male prepares and cleans a site in the sand, upon which the female lays one hundred to five hundred eggs. After fertilization, both parents participate in the cleaning and fanning of the eggs and both care for the brood after hatching. Both parents spit out chewed-up food for the young.

Fire mouths require large tanks and do well in community aquariums as long as their tankmates do not harass them. If annoyed, they will become aggressive in order to defend themselves. The aquarium should have open space for swimming as well as rocks for shelter.

The fire mouth prefers live foods such as daphnia, tubifex worms, brine shrimp, and insect larvae, and water temperatures between 68° and 75° F (20°–24° C) for most of the year. During the mating season, temperatures should be raised to 79° F (26° C).

Angel Fish (Pterophyllum scalare)

Family Cichlidae

Unrelated to the marine angel fishes, these freshwater cichlids of the Amazon have a distinctive shape and long fins. They have been among the most popular aquarium fishes since they were first imported in the early 1900s, and several new varieties have been bred in captivity. Its beauty and the ease with which it is maintained make this species one of the beginning aquarist's favorites. Specimens have lived in home aquariums for more than twelve years.

The angel fish's body is deep, disc-shaped, compressed, and has a symmetrical appearance because of the long, sickle-shaped, nearly equal-sized dorsal and anal fins. The ventral fins, also long, appear to be threadlike filaments. The body may reach five and a half inches (14 cm) in length, and its color ranges from silver to gray-green, with a brownish undertone. There are four vertical black bars, only one of which is really distinct. The remaining three fade and reappear with stress and environmental changes. The dorsal and anal fins are blue-gray and are lighter at the tip.

The species prefers water temperatures of 75°–79° F (24°–26° C) and well-planted tanks. The broad, ribbonlike leaves of aquatic plants such as *Vallisneria, Myriophyllum,* and *Sagittaria* are used in spawning. Courting and reproduction patterns are similar to those of the genus *Haplochromis,* and both parents clean and fan the eggs. After hatching, the young remain attached to the plant leaves by means of an adhesive mechanism.

Discus (Symphosodon discus)

Family Cichlidae

These eight-inch-long (20.3-cm) disc-shaped freshwater fish inhabit the entire Amazon drainage system from Peru and Venezuela to the mouth of the river. They occur where plants grow profusely in quiet backwaters and bends and pools in the river. Discus are remarkable because of the very specialized care they give their young. Behavior during courtship and

◀ Angel fish ▼ Discus

reproduction and care of the eggs prior to hatching are similar to those of the angel fish. However, after the eggs hatch, the adults exhibit a care pattern not seen in any other fish. The young attach to the adults and feed on a protein secretion on the skin of the parent. If one parent does not have enough of this food substance, the young shift to the other parent, and at times can be seen moving back and forth as the parents divide the feeding responsibilities. After a few weeks of feeding in this manner, the young begin to feed independently.

Several discus varieties have been identified; most are probably distinct geographic populations or races of the single species *Symphysodon discus*. Color varies widely with local habitat and geographic race, and even within the same variety color changes occur with changes in behavior. The basic pattern consists of fifteen to eighteen horizontal red-brown and blue streaks which begin behind the gill and end at the base of the dorsal and anal fins. In addition there are usually nine vertical bars, three of which are dark blue. The first bar, which runs through the eyes, forms an oblique stripe on the cheek; the dorsal and anal fins are edged in light blue and have scattered spots; the pectoral fin is light blue.

131

Family Pomacentridae: Clown Fishes and Damsel Fishes

Members of this family are typically small and brilliantly colored, and live among the tropical coral reefs of the Atlantic, Pacific, and Indian oceans. Only a few Indo-Australian species are known to invade fresh or brackish water. In addition to being small, these fishes have short heads and compressed bodies covered with ctenoid scales. The mouth is small, and poorly developed teeth are present in the jaws only. The dorsal fins are not divided, and the spiny portion is shorter than the soft rays. The anal fin contains two or three spiny rays. Like the cichlids, pomacentrids have a single opening on each side of the nose.

Generally these fishes live in pairs or small groups in and around coral reefs. Only members of the genus *Chromis* form large schools and live in open water above the reefs. Most are diurnal, hiding in crevices at night and taking on a different coloration—frequently the reverse of their daytime coloration—when they sleep. Color changes also occur in the males during the breeding season.

Damsel fishes are nest builders and provide parental care for the eggs and young. The male generally prepares the nest and does a peculiar loping dance to attract females. Several females may nest and spawn with one male, but after spawning they are all driven off and care of the young is completed by the male. Many males are very territorial and aggressive, and not only during the breeding season. One Pacific species that lives off the California-Mexico coast, the Garibaldi *(Hypsypops rubicunda)*, which attains a length of nearly twelve inches (30.5 cm), will even attempt to drive scuba divers away from the nest. This pugnacious behavior restricts the number of species suitable for aquarium display.

The best-known members of the family are the clown fishes, or anemone fishes, which inhabit the Indo-Pacific region exclusively. All twenty-six clown fish species resemble one another in their rust-red body coloration and white stripes. All species have been successfully maintained in aquariums and many have been bred in captivity.

In the wild, clown fishes are always found near anemone, with which they live in a mutualistic relationship. They secrete a compound through their skin that either inhibits the release of the anemone's stinging cells or provides protection from the poison released by those cells. Clown fishes swim freely among the anemone's poisonous tentacles, which provide an ideal sanctuary from predators—any other fish that comes too close is immediately stung and perhaps killed. Small specimens, less than one inch, rarely leave the disc area of the anemone. Adults will venture a few meters away, always dashing back when threatened.

There is some evidence that these fishes not only obtain protection from the anemone but also feed on its excreta or nibble its tentacles. In aquariums, clown fishes have also been observed feeding the anemone, an activity that may occur only rarely in the wild and may in fact be an attempt by the fish to store food. Clown fishes have been known to "feed" large bits of food to the "holes" in coral when an anemone is unavailable.

Clown Fish or Anemone Fish (Amphiprion ocellaris)
Family Pomacentridae

This species is the most common representative of the genus imported for the marine hobbyist. For many years it was mis-identified as Amphiprion percula, which has a restricted distribution through the New Hebrides, the Solomon Islands, New Guinea, and Queensland, Australia. A. ocellaris has a much wider distribution throughout the Indo-Pacific and can be distinguished by the presence of eleven dorsal spines. A. percula has only nine or ten dorsal spines, and the black edging around the white bars on its body is much broader.

A. ocellaris has the orange color typical of all clown fishes, and it has three white bars edged in black. The dorsal, anal, pectoral, pelvic, and caudal fins are also edged in black.

This species has been maintained in aquariums for many years and is one of the few marine fishes that has been **133** spawned in captivity. After the substrate has been cleaned by the male, the female will lay up to two hundred eggs. These are tended by the male for about seven days, until they hatch. The young, immediately free-swimming and in no need of care, quickly migrate to the surface, where they remain for a few weeks. Eventually they settle to the bottom.

Very few anemone fishes can be considered schooling types, but A. ocellaris young group together in small schools and several individuals may inhabit a single anemone. Although they can get along in the aquarium without one another, the fish and the anemone do better in captivity when both are present.

Clown fish are good specimens for beginning hobbyists, since aquarium care for the species is relatively simple. Water temperature should be kept above 74° F (23° C), and the fish's diet should consist of live or frozen brine shrimp, or chopped fish and shrimp. The anemone will do well on the same diet.

Clown fish

Three-spot Damsel Fish *(Dascyllus albisella)*

Family Pomacentridae

Some members of this genus are striped and others spotted, but all are black and white. They live among the corals and gorgoniums of the tropical reefs, and many live only with one species of coral.

The three-spot damsel inhabits the Hawaiian Islands and is closely related to *D. trimaculatis* of the Indo-Pacific. It differs from the latter species in having a much larger white spot on its side. These are elegant swimmers, not as territorial as other members of the family.

Three-spot damsels adapt to aquarium life quickly and completely, spending most of their time swimming about the open space, and retiring at night to secluded corners and crevices to sleep. In captivity they do not require the specific coral they live with in the wild, though it is a good idea to furnish the tank with some coral for the fish to shelter in. Water temperature should be maintained above 74° F (23° C), and the diet may consist of finely chopped shrimp or fish or live or frozen brine shrimp.

135

Three-spot damsel fish

Beau Gregory (*Eupomacentrus leucostictus*)

Family Pomacentridae

Although this fish is known as a seasonal visitor to Cape Cod and Maine, its common habitat is the tropical reefs of the western Atlantic. Beau Gregories reach approximately four inches (10 cm) in length and are interesting additions to the aquarium because of their continuous movement and their bright yellow-and-blue coloration. These fish are quite territorial and only one or two specimens can be maintained in a single tank.

These aggressive fish are well known for their fin-nipping behavior and should not be placed in the same tank with such peaceful species as banner fish and moorish idols. They are also tough fish—they can withstand poor environmental conditions better than many other tropical marine fishes. However, pollution and improper salinity and temperature will cause the fish to be less active and will dull their colors. Ideally, the water should be very clean and the temperature above 74° F (23° C). Beau Gregories feed on plankton in the wild; in captivity they do well on live or frozen brine shrimp.

Beau Gregory

Labroidei: Wrasses

Wrasses are brightly colored fishes that inhabit all tropical, subtropical, and temperate seas. Juveniles, adult males, and females often have individual color phases, making it difficult to identify some species.

Wrasses have perchlike bodies covered with cycloid scales. The mouth is generally small and may be protruded, with one or more rows of canine teeth in the jaws. Some species have a strong tooth located inside the mouth which is used for crushing mussel and snail shells.

Wrasses are quick swimmers, and while some are solitary, many are found in schools. The tail provides propulsion during fast swimming, and the pectoral fins are stroked alternately when the fishes are swimming slowly.

There are more than sixty genera and over six hundred species of wrasses. Some care for their young and build nests on the bottom, and many species build nests for sleeping each night. Wrasses generally feed on a variety of bottom-dwelling organisms such as snails, mussels, and crabs.

Clown Wrasse *(Coris gaimardi)*

Family Labridae

A common inhabitant of the tropical Indo-Pacific reefs, clown wrasses are found from Africa east to Hawaii. Although not aggressive toward other species, the six-inch-long (15.2-cm) adults will fight with one another over territories. Their tiny mouths contain sharp and protruding canine teeth; normally used to capture invertebrate prey, in the aquarium they can sometimes remove scales from tankmates.

The juvenile clown wrasse is bright red or orange with black-edged white spots. After reaching half its adult length, it begins undergoing a transformation that ultimately yields a fish so different in appearance that many scientists once believed two distinct species existed. As the clown wrasse grows, the red fades and the tail yellows, until maturity renders a blue adult with red spots and a bright yellow tail.

Many aquarists have discovered upon bringing a clown **137**

Clown wrasse adult ▲ and juvenile ▼

wrasse home that their new pet soon disappeared, only to reappear a few days later. This disappearing act is a protective mechanism—once they have acclimated to new surroundings, clown wrasses burrow into the sand each night to sleep and to avoid predators.

Sometimes these fish suffer shock from handling and upon arriving lie on their sides at the bottom and appear to be breathing hard. At this time the best treatment is to leave the fish alone, increase the aeration, and darken the tank. Generally the wrasse will be swimming normally in a few hours.

Cleaner Wrasse or Barberfish (Labroides dimidiatus)

Family Labridae

Members of the genus *Labroides* are best known for their symbiotic relationships with other fishes. Their diet consists mainly of the parasites living on the bodies and in the gill and mouth cavities of other fishes such as groupers, moray eels, snappers, and butterfly fishes. All *Labroides* species show adaptations for their specialized diets, such as pointed snouts and forcepslike teeth. Their bright colors and striking patterns, in sharp contrast to their surroundings, are believed to serve as ''advertisements'' to the fishes they associate with.

Juvenile *Labroides* are generally dark or black. As they mature, a striped pattern develops which may be blue, brown, or yellow, depending on the species. *L. dimidiatus*, the most common aquarium species, has a blue pattern. The mid-strip runs from the tip of the snout to the tail and is nearly black. The body color is almost sky-blue.

Cleaner wrasses were first observed in the early 1950s when aqualung-equipped scientists ventured below the sea to learn how fishes live. Some of these scientists observed that many fishes gathered at specific locations and appeared to be waiting in line for ''barbering.'' The barberfish would proceed to remove offending parasites or clean festering wounds. Before the tiny barber approaches potential predators, the fish wanting cleaning positions itself near the coral, extends its gill covers, and opens its mouth to indicate that it will not eat its servant. Cleaning behavior has been observed in a number of other families, and some Caribbean gobies have color patterns nearly identical to that of the cleaner wrasse.

The cleaner wrasse does well in home aquariums and will display cleaning behavior in captivity. Brine shrimp and finely chopped fish or shrimp adequately replace the parasite diet.

Like many other wrasses, these fish will disappear at night. They do not burrow into the sand but secrete a mucous cocoon around themselves which mutes their bright colors. As further camouflage, debris sticks to the surface of the cocoon, making detection quite difficult.

139

◄ Cleaner wrasse on moray eel

Bluehead Wrasse (Thalassoma bifasciatum)

Family Labridae

The bluehead, one of the more abundant reef fishes of the Caribbean, has several color phases and two separate reproductive patterns.

Young blueheads have a black mid-lateral stripe, with yellow above and white below the stripe, and there are pale red blotches on the head. During this period of their lives they grow to two inches (5 cm) and become sexually mature. Courtship and spawning are group activities; the floating eggs are released by the females and fertilized by the males as the entire school swims from the bottom to the surface. When the fish reach five inches (12.7 cm) the color pattern changes: the black stripe breaks up into a series of faint square blotches, or it may disappear entirely, leaving the body completely yellow. Growth for the females and most males ceases at this point. About 5 percent of the males, however, continue to grow, and they begin a transformation that eventually yields a fish with a bright blue head and a green body crossed by two vertical black bars separated by a light blue interspace. These males mate with the yellow females, courting individual females and forming distinct pairs—spawning no longer occurs as a group activity. (Because of their striking coloration and their courtship behavior, these males are sometimes called "super

Bluehead wrasse

males.'') Bluehead wrasses have not spawned in captivity, and although the size of the fish is known for each part of the life cycle, the age at which each phase begins has not been determined.

In the aquarium, blueheads accept brine shrimp and chopped fish in lieu of their normal diet of plankton. Like other wrasses, they disappear at night and burrow in the sand to sleep.

Trachinoidei: Weevers, Sandfishes, and Jawfishes

Yellowhead Jawfish *(Opistognathus aurifrons)*
Family Opistognathidae

The suborder Trachinoidei contains sixteen little-known families, of which only the jawfishes are maintained in aquariums. Some are deep-sea forms, while others are venomous inshore dwellers.

Jawfishes are found in tropical seas throughout the world. The most familiar species, the yellowhead, is also the prettiest. An inhabitant of the reefs of Florida and the West Indies, this four-inch-long (10-cm) species adds interest as well as color to the aquarium. Its large head and short snout are accentuated by large blue eyes. The body is pale blue with numerous blue spots, and the head and nape are bright yellow.

In the aquarium, jawfishes must be provided with sand and

Yellowhead jawfish

small rocks so they can construct burrows. Each individual constructs a vertical burrow lined with stones or pieces of shell, and this becomes its exclusive territory. The fish waits for food in the area above the burrow, and darts back inside at the first sign of danger. Yellowheads are particularly territorial and will steal rocks and shells from neighbors' burrows. Fatal fights may occur if too many yellowheads are placed in one tank, or if they are prevented from constructing burrows.

All jawfishes are carnivorous and feed on plankton in the wild. In captivity they accept chopped fish, shrimp, and live or frozen brine shrimp. Yellowheads have not been bred in captivity, and little is known of their reproductive patterns. Some jawfishes are known to be mouth brooders, with the male caring for the eggs and young.

Gobioidei: Gobies

Neon Goby (Gobiosoma oceanops)
Family Gobiidae

Gobies constitute the largest family (more than one thousand species) of temperate and tropical fishes. They are the smallest fishes, as well as the smallest vertebrates. The dwarf pygmy goby (Pandaka pygmaea) attains a length of only three-eighths of an inch (9.5 mm). Most gobies are carnivorous bottom-dwellers, and their pelvic fins are joined to form a sucking disc. Many species live in brackish water and a few live in fresh water. Some freshwater forms return to the sea to spawn.

The neon goby's life style and appearance are nearly identical to those of the cleaner wrasses of the Pacific, though the species are unrelated and live half a world apart. This blue-and-white goby of Florida and the Yucatan and other members of the genus inhabiting the Caribbean and the Bahamas are the primary cleaner fishes of the region. In captivity, Pacific fishes accept cleaning from these gobies even though they would never encounter them in nature.

One or more of these gobies may inhabit a coral head together, all providing barbering services. More than fifty-four

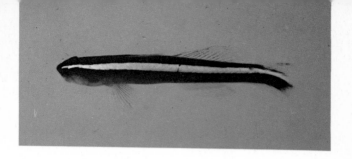

species of fishes in Florida have been observed being cleaned. Unlike the wrasses, which swim and hover about the host, neon gobies attach themselves to the fish being cleaned by their sucking disk. Some "cleaning stations" have been occupied by gobies continuously for two years.

Reproduction occurs from January to May. The male prepares a nesting site and initiates courtship. During mating the male displays for the female with a quivering side-to-side dance. After the eggs are laid, the male guards the nest for twelve to eighteen days, until the eggs hatch. Neon gobies have been bred in captivity, but successful rearing of the young has been limited.

In aquariums neon gobies readily accept live brine shrimp in lieu of parasites. At night they appear to prefer the protection of live corals for sleeping.

Acanthuroidei: Surgeon Fishes

Surgeon fishes are marine fishes with deep, compressed, oval-shaped bodies. The common name is derived from the modified scales located near the tail on the sides of the caudal peduncle. These scales resemble scalpels and are indeed used for cutting. The rest of the body and the head are covered with small rough scales, and the mouth contains a single row of teeth in each jaw. Surgeon fishes' food preferences range from algae to plankton and are reflected in the shapes of the specialized teeth, which may be cupped, caninelike, two-pointed, or brushlike.

One of the suborder's distinguishing features is its larvae, which have vertical ridges. After the eggs hatch, the young remain in a larval stage for five days. During this phase they are carnivorous and feed on small crustaceans and fish eggs. **143**

Neon goby

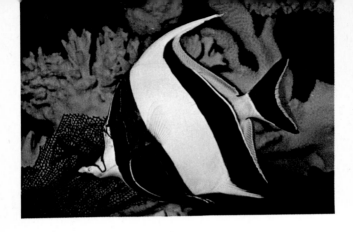

Moorish Idol *(Zanclus canescens)*

Family Acanthuridae

The moorish idol's dazzling coloration, disc shape, long dorsal fin, and projecting mouth resemble those of the banner fish. The resemblance may even confuse the fishes themselves, for mixed schools are seen on the reef, and the two species are extremely compatible in captivity. Moorish idols, found throughout the tropical Indo-Pacific from Africa to Mexico, are included in the surgeon fish family because they go through the characteristic larval phase.

Moorish idols are a difficult species to maintain, and little is known of their habits in the wild. They appear to live in pairs, but schools of a hundred are frequently seen. Nothing is known of their breeding behavior—the larvae are pelagic, and young fish simply appear around the reef. Their teeth are apparently adapted for scraping algae or small animals off the substrate, but the actual components of their diet in the wild are not known. At Marineland of the Pacific, a few specimens were kept for more than three years on finely ground squid, shrimp, and fish, plus spinach and live brine shrimp. Many home aquarists, however, have a hard time feeding moorish idols, for they are fussy eaters in captivity. Often they will appear to eat large quantities of food, yet they become emaciated and gradually starve to death or succumb to disease. Still, despite the difficulty of maintaining this species, the

moorish idol remains a favorite with marine aquarists.

Moorish idol

Smoothhead Surgeon Fish *(Naso lituratus)*
Family Acanthuridae

Just in front of the caudal fin, on the side of the caudal peduncle, surgeon fishes have modified scales which are sharp as
knives. In some species the "knives" are immovable, but in
others they are retractable, resembling switchblades. In all
species they are quite sharp and can inflict serious wounds on
other fishes or people.

The smoothhead surgeon belongs to a genus popularly
known as unicorn fishes, characterized by fixed tail knives and
horns projecting from the forehead. The smoothhead is
probably the most attractive member of the genus. Its most
striking features are the filaments that trail from the upper and
lower lobes of the caudal fin, and its contrasting colors: blue
dorsal fin, black back band, red anal fin, and yellow head and
abdomen. The blue-and-white-spotted young are not as colorful as the adults.

All surgeon fishes are herbivorous and have teeth adapted
for scraping algae off rocks and coral. If possible, algae should
be permitted to grow in the tank, or chopped spinach substi-
tuted for algae to ensure a healthy diet.

No more than two smoothheads should be kept in the
average tank. These fish establish social hierarchies, and the
dominant member will chase subordinates until all are
exhausted or wounded. Very little is known about the breeding habits of these fish, and they have not spawned in captivity.

Smoothhead surgeon fish

Flagtail Tang *or* Blue Surgeon Fish *(Paracanthurus hepatus)*
Family Acanthuridae

Natives of the Indo-Pacific, flagtail tangs have been imported to the United States regularly since 1968. Their unique black, blue, and yellow coloration accounts in large measure for their popularity.

Like other surgeons, the flagtail tang has sharp modified scales on the caudal peduncle. In this species, as in several others that are schooling fishes, the knives are not large nor are they used against schoolmates. In the ocean, schools of flagtails may contain hundreds or even thousands of fish. This species is one of the ideal members of its family for the home aquarium. Two or three individuals get along well together in a thirty-gallon community tank.

Flagtail tangs are herbivorous and do well on a regular diet of chopped fish, shrimp, and live brine shrimp, supplemented with chopped spinach. Water temperature should be maintained near 78° F (25.5° C).

Anabantoidei: Labyrinth Fishes, Climbing Perches, and Gouramis

This suborder of Perciformes is distinguished from other fishes by the presence of the "labyrinth," a cavelike auxiliary breathing organ located on either side of the head above the gill cavity. These chambers are outgrowths of the ordinary branchial chambers and contain a rosettelike structure made up of a number of bony plates. Each of these air reservoirs connects with the branchial chamber and the throat. A special valve admits air to the chamber for the throat during swallow-**146** ing, and used air is expelled through the gill openings. So

Flagtail tang ▲ Paradise fish ▶

important is this method of respiration that many labyrinth fishes suffocate or drown if denied access to the surface. Newly hatched members of this suborder depend on their gills for respiration for only a few days.

Paradise Fish (Macropodus opercularis)
Family Belontiidae

Paradise and fighting fishes were probably the first live tropical fishes imported to Europe. The fish arrived in France in 1869 from a stock bred in captivity for many years in their native eastern Asia.

Paradise fish have oblong, flattened bodies that reach three inches (7.6 cm) in length. They have large heads, small up-turned mouths, and large, long dorsal and anal fins. Native fish are green-brown with a dark brown to purple back. Parts of the body are red to bright crimson with blue-green stripes, and the edge of the gill cover is fire-red with a black spot.

During the mating season the male builds a nest of bubbles beneath floating plant leaves. The males make the bubbles by holding air in the mouth and secreting a sticky saliva around it. Courtship includes U-shaped embraces by the male and female. After fertilization, the female will lay one hundred to five hundred eggs, most of which float into the nest. Those that sink are picked up by the male and placed in the nest. After spawning the male drives the female away and tends the nest. The eggs hatch in thirty-six to forty-eight hours.

Paradise fish are easy to care for and are popular with beginning aquarists. For breeding, the temperature must be at least 70°–73° F (21°–23° C), even though they will live comfortably in temperatures as low as 59° F(15°C).

Siamese Fighting Fish *(Betta splendens)*

Family Belontiidae

The family Belontiidae takes its name from the Latin word for "warrior," and indeed fighting fish are aggressive toward their own kind. In their native waters of Southeast Asia these fish establish territories that keep the males separated and allow the losers to escape. However, in a small aquarium this territorial behavior results in death to the vanquished. In Thailand and Singapore these fish are regularly exhibited in public fights and provide the basis of a public "sport."

Siamese fighting fish were first brought to Europe in 1874 and bred there in 1893. The wild fish live in freshwater ditches and rice paddies and differ considerably from the "domesticated" aquarium types. In the northern parts of their native waters these fish are greenish, and in the southern parts they are reddish. Several varieties exist and until recently each was considered a separate species. By selective- and crossbreeding techniques many beautiful varieties have been developed, including all-red, green, and long-finned and large-tailed forms. Females are not as brightly colored and are smaller than the males.

The slender body of the fighting fish barely exceeds two and a half inches (6.4 cm) in length. They have a pointed snout, an upturned mouth, and large fins. The dorsal fin is located near the rear of the body, and the rounded caudal fin is joined to the anal fin, which runs from the tail to near the pelvic fins and gills.

Although aquarium requirements for Siamese fighting fish are simple, they are not ideal community fish. If kept with their own kind, males will fight even juveniles and immature females. If kept with other fishes, they will not develop brilliant colors. Many hobbyists prefer to hold the males in small individual containers, which permits the males to see one another. This visual contact stimulates territoriality and sexual development of breeding colors without permitting fights.

These fish will survive in any container as long as there is
148 water to swim in. Since they are labyrinth breathers, they do

not require aeration. They are omnivorous and accept all kinds of food. Temperature is the most important factor in their survival; it must be maintained above 75° F (24° C) and at 86° F (30° C) for breeding.

Successful breeding requires clean, thickly planted tanks with floating plants for bubble-nest building. Courtship is aggressive; males pursue females by nipping at their fins, and females often try to escape. When ready to spawn, the pair turn over with abdomens together. Upon release, the eggs are immediately fertilized, and the male picks them up in his mouth and deposits them in the nest. After the eggs hatch in thirty to forty hours the parents should be kept away, otherwise they may eat the young. Fighting fish attain maturity in three months and live for about one year.

149

Siamese fighting fish

Pearl Gourami *(Trichogaster leeri)*

Family Belontiidae

Unlike paradise and fighting fishes, gouramis have a specialized pelvic fin ray that contains tactile sensory cells. It is used to touch other members of the species for identification and environmental objects for awareness.

Gouramis are the largest labyrinth breathers, and some species grow to more than a foot long (30.5 cm). The pearl gourami is a small species, rarely exceeding five inches (12.7 cm). Its body is oval and has a tapered head. It has a long anal fin, a short but high dorsal fin, and the caudal fin has two lobes. Generally, the body is blue with white spots. The chest and anal and pelvic fins are red and the dorsal fin is blue-edged. Its colors intensify during the breeding season. Males tend to be larger than females, with longer dorsal fins.

Native to Thailand and Borneo, pearl gouramis live in waters thick with plants and in stagnant ponds. They are easy to maintain in captivity, and are more peaceful than most labyrinth fishes. They require a minimum temperature of 68° F (20° C) to survive and about 74° F (23° C) to reproduce. They will accept nearly every type of live and prepared food.

Like most members of their family, they are bubble-nest builders. Because plant material is incorporated into the nest, the aquarium should contain fine-leafed plants. Eggs hatch after twenty-four hours, and the young remain in the nest for three days. As the young swarm from the nest, it breaks up.

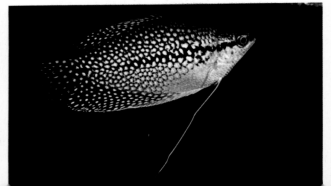

Kissing Gourami *(Helostoma temmincki)*
Family Helostomatidae

These natives of the marshes in Borneo, Sumatra, and Thailand are classified in a separate family of labyrinth fishes because of the structure and attachment of certain head bones, the lack of teeth in the jaws, and the presence of thick protrusile lips. Kissing gouramis also have well-developed gill rakers for plankton feeding.

These rather drab-colored fish have become aquarium favorites because of their kissing behavior. In this species, kissing has nothing to do with courtship behavior. It occurs only between males, as a nonviolent form of aggression used to establish social dominance and territory.

Courtship and mating occur after the rainy season in the flooded marshes, where decaying plants provide ample nutrients for the infusoria upon which the young fish feed. Females initiate breeding and may be followed by several males. After spawning, the eggs float to the surface and hatch within forty-eight hours. The species has been bred in captivity, and the only difficulty occurs in feeding the young, which need small food particles during the first days of life. Adults accept nearly any prepared foods and scrape algae off the walls and aquatic plants of the tank. **151**

◄ Pearl gourami ▲ Kissing gouramis

Tetraodontiformes: Triggerfishes and Puffers

Tetraodontiformes, an order thought to be related to the surgeon fishes, is divided into two suborders: triggerfishes (Balistoidei) and puffers (Tetraodontoidei).

Triggerfishes are colorful tropical fishes that received their name from the unique locking apparatus of the dorsal fin. The function of this fin is protective, for when triggerfishes wedge themselves into holes and crevices and erect this dorsal fin, it is nearly impossible to extricate them unless the mechanism is depressed and unlocked. When the fin is raised, the base of the second spine holds the first erect, and when the muscle attached to the third spine contracts it unlocks the mechanism. The pelvic fins are reduced to a single spiny knob which is used for leverage. Triggerfishes swim by undulating the soft dorsal and anal fins. Although they have small mouths, their jaws contain close-set, protruding teeth which are often reinforced by inner teeth. This allows them to feed on hard-shelled crabs, mollusks, echinoderms, and even coral.

Puffers are best known for their ability to double their size by inflating their bodies by swallowing water or air, a defense mechanism that protects them from predators. Ordinarily they swallow water; air is ingested only by accident or after capture, and has no biological advantage. The ingested water is pumped into a special sac off the stomach beneath the viscera.

Puffers can be found in warm temperate and tropical seas. They generally have round bodies, and the tough skin often has sharp spines which erect when the body is inflated. Their fused teeth form a strong beak which can break tough shells or coral. The first dorsal and pelvic fins are absent; the second dorsal, anal, and pectoral fins are well developed. Puffers can move backward and forward equally well.

Clown Triggerfish (Balistoides niger)
Family Balistidae

One of the most prized aquarium species, clown triggerfish have commanded high prices since the early 1960s, when they were introduced to hobbyists. If not the most unusual

species, it competes for that distinction with lion fishes, blue surgeon fish, moorish idols, and bat fish. It is not abundant anywhere in its range, which extends from Africa to the Philippine archipelago. The brilliant colors and unique pattern of this fish are important for species recognition, allowing individuals to maintain geographic territories without combat.

The skin has regular rows of close-set but movable bony plates. On the caudal peduncle the plates have a series of spiny ridges similar to the knifelike scales of surgeon fishes. The first spine of the dorsal fin trigger mechanism is the largest, and its front edge is as rough as a rasp. The second and third spines are smooth. The teeth, typical of triggerfishes, make a noise when scraped together.

The clown triggerfish is a solitary species, and only one or two should be kept together. In addition to being aggressive to its own kind, it is a fin nipper and should not be kept with small, gentle fishes. This species grows to twelve inches in length (30.5 cm); specimens smaller than four inches (10 cm) have not been discovered. It is believed that juveniles may be another color or live in very deep water.

In captivity clown triggerfish readily accept animal matter and starfish, sea urchins, and live shrimp. They prefer water temperatures near 80° F (27° C), and most aquarists keep them in a tank decorated to simulate a coral reef. **153**

Clown triggerfish

Fantail Filefish *(Pervagor spilosoma)*
Family Balistidae
In many texts filefishes are listed in a separate family, Monocanthidae, and because they lack the dorsal fin trigger mechanism are not included with triggerfishes. However, other anatomical similarities, including bone structure, tooth formation, and scales, indicate a close relationship. Their common name refers not to the spiny dorsal fin, but to the rough texture of the skin, which is as abrasive as sandpaper. It contains numerous small scales, and on some parts of the body, particularly near the tail, each scale has a minute spiny projection.

The body of the filefish is compressed and thin. There are no pectoral fins, and a ridge runs from the throat to the anal fin. There is a single spine on the belly. The mouth is tiny, and the jaws have six pairs of teeth. The caudal fin is large, and as the fish swims it is alternately opened and closed, giving the appearance of an old-fashioned fan.

An omnivorous fish, this species inhabits shallow water in the tropical Pacific from the East Indies to Hawaii. Very little is known about its reproductive habits. The eggs and larvae float near the surface and are pelagic, drifting with the ocean currents. Both adults and young are nonaggressive and do well in the aquarium. Their diet should contain both plant and animal material, although they will survive on chopped fish, shrimp and brine shrimp. The temperature should be maintained between 74° and 80° F (23°–27° C).

Fantail filefish

Spiny Puffer *or* Porcupine Fish *(Diodon hystrix)*

Family Diodontidae

Like its mammalian namesake, this species has skin covered with spines which it can erect or depress at will. When the porcupine fish is faced with danger, it will also swallow water and inflate its body, causing the spines to protrude at right angles to the body and making it virtually impossible for any would-be predator to get too close.

This fish's body is nearly globular, its head is rounded, and the teeth in its small mouth are fused. The dorsal and anal fins are opposite one another and provide the primary propulsion for swimming.

Unlike other members of the puffer family, porcupine fish do not have a special inflation sac. Water for inflating the body is ingested and held within the stomach. The fish deflates by contracting the body muscles and regurgitating the water.

Porcupine fish are distributed throughout the warm waters of the world, though they are more common in bays and mangrove marshes than around coral reefs. Primarily nocturnal, they feed on sea urchins, crabs, and mollusks. They often blow water into the sand to dig out buried shellfish. In the aquarium they become quite tame and will wait at the surface to be fed. Often they blow water out of the tank while waiting. They do well in temperatures from 68° to 80° F (20°−27°C).

Porcupine fish

Selected Bibliography

Amlacher, Erwin. *Textbook of Fish Diseases*. Neptune City, N.J.: T.F.H. Publications, 1970.

Axelrod, Herbert R., and Emmens, Clifford W. *Exotic Marine Fishes*. Neptune City, N.J.: T.F.H. Publications, 1975.

Axelrod, Herbert R., Vorderwinkler, W., *et al. Exotic Tropical Fishes*. Neptune City, N.J.: T.F.H. Publications, 1962.

Bellomy, Mildred D. and M. Y. *Encyclopedia of Sea Horses*. Neptune City, N.J.: T.F.H. Publications, 1969.

Greenwood, P.H., and Norman, J.R. *A History of Fishes,* 3rd ed. New York: Halsted Press, 1975.

Grzimek, Bernhard. *Grzimek's Animal Life Encyclopedia*. Vol. 4: Fishes 1; Vol. 5: Fishes 2 and Amphibians. New York: Van Nostrand Reinhold, 1973–74.

Herald, Earl S. *Living Fishes of the World*. New York: Doubleday, 1961.

Hoedeman, J. J. *Naturalists' Guide to Fresh-Water Aquarium Fish*. New York: Sterling, 1974.

Madsen, J. M. *Aquarium Fishes in Color*. New York: Macmillan, 1975.

Nieuwenhuizen, De Graas Vander. *Marine Aquarium Guide*. New York: Doubleday, 1974.

Reichenbach-Klinke, H., and Elkan, E. *The Principle Diseases of Lower Vertebrates*. Book 1: *Diseases of Fishes*. London: Academic Press, 1965.

Sterba, Gunther. *Sterba's Freshwater Fishes of the World*. 2 vols. Neptune City, N.J.: T.F.H. Publications, 1974.

World Aquariums

United States of America

T: Wayland Vaughan Aquarium, La Jolla, California

Marineland of the Pacific, Palos Verdes, California

Sea World, San Diego, California

Steinhart Aquarium, San Francisco, California

Mystic Marinelife Aquarium, Mystic, Connecticut

National Aquarium, Washington, D.C.

National Zoological Park, Washington, D.C.

Miami Seaquarium, Miami, Florida

Sea World Florida, Orlando, Florida

Marineland, St. Augustine, Florida

Waikiki Aquarium, Honolulu, Oahu, Hawaii

Sea Life Park, Waimanalo, Oahu, Hawaii

John G. Shedd Aquarium, Chicago, Illinois

New England Aquarium, Boston, Massachusetts

National Marine Fisheries Service, Woods Hole, Massachusetts

New York Aquarium, Brooklyn, New York

Aquarium of Niagara Falls, Niagara Falls, New York

Sea World Ohio, Aurora, Ohio

Cleveland Aquarium, Cleveland, Ohio

The Dallas Aquarium, Dallas, Texas

Australia

Sea World of Australia, Surfers Paradise, Brisbane

Taronga Zoo and Aquarium, Sydney

Belgium

Aquarium of the Royal Zoological Society, Antwerp

Canada

Montreal Aquarium, Montreal, Quebec

Marineland and Game Farm, Niagara Falls, Ontario

Vancouver Public Aquarium, Vancouver, British Columbia

Czechoslovakia

Zoo-Aqua-terra, Pilsen

Denmark

Danmarks Akvarium, • Charlottenlund

France

Aquarium de la Ménagerie, Paris

German Democratic Republic (East Germany)

Aquarium and Terrarium of Tierpark Berlin, East Berlin

Germany, West

Aquarium of the Berliner Zoo, West Berlin

Wilhelma Aquarium, Stuttgart

Great Britain

The Aquarium, Plymouth

Iran

Tehran Zoological Gardens, Tehran

Israel

Marine Museum-Aquarium, Eilat

Italy

Aquarium, Naples

Japan

Enoshima Aquarium, Marineland, Marinezoo, Fujisawa

Ueono Zoo Aquarium, Tokyo

Yomiuri Land Marine Aquarium, Tokyo

Monaco

Aquarium du Musée Océanographique

Netherlands

Artis-Aquarium, Amsterdam

New Caledonia

Aquarium de Nouméa, Nouméa

New Zealand

Hawke's Bay Aquarium, Napier

Marineland of New Zealand, Napier

Norway

Akvariet i Bergen, Bergen

Poland

Akwarium, Lodz

Spain

Acuario de la Barcelona, Barcelona

Sweden

Nordiska Museet and Skansen, Stockholm

Switzerland

Aquarium of the Zoological Park, Bern

USSR

Aquarium of the Moscow Zoo, Moscow

Aquarium of the Institute of Biology of the South Seas, Sevastopol

Index

John H. Prescott is Executive Director and Vice-President of the New England Aquarium in Boston, Massachusetts. The author of numerous articles on fishes and marine mammals, he has also served as General Manager of Marineland of the Pacific in Palos Verdes, California, and is a Corporator of the Woods Hole Oceanographic Institution, Woods Hole, Massachusetts.